Harro von Senger

The
36
Stratagems
for Business

Harro von Senger

The
36
Stratagems
for Business

Achieve your objectives through hidden and
unconventional strategies and tactics

CYAN

 Marshall Cavendish
Business

Authorized translation from the original German language edition published as *36 Strategeme für Manager* by Carl Hanser Verlag, Munich/FRG, 2004

English translation copyright © 2006 by Marshall Cavendish (Asia) Private Limited

This translation first published in 2006 by:

Marshall Cavendish Business

An imprint of Marshall Cavendish International (Asia) Private Limited
A member of Times Publishing Limited
Times Centre, 1 New Industrial Road
Singapore 536196

T: +65 6213 9300
F: +65 6285 4871
E: te@sg.marshallcavendish.com
Online bookstore: www.marshallcavendish.com/genref

and

Cyan Communications Limited
119 Wardour Street
London W1F 0UW
United Kingdom

T: +44 (0)20 7565 6120
E: sales@cyanbooks.com
www.cyanbooks.com

A CIP record for this book is available from the British Library

ISBN-13 978 981 261 814 6 (Asia & ANZ)
ISBN-10 981 261 814 7 (Asia & ANZ)
ISBN 1-904879-46-2 (Rest of world)

Translated and typeset by Cambridge Publishing Management Limited, United Kingdom (Translators: Vivien Groves, John Kelly, Michele McMeekin, Tess Pike, and James Taylor.)

Printed and bound in Singapore

Acknowledgments

For valuable suggestions based on reading some or all of the manuscript, I should like to thank Professor Manfred Gross of the Chinese–German College, Tongji University, Shanghai, formerly deputy director of corporate human resources, Siemens AG; academic director Dr. Klaus Kammerer of the Faculty of Economic and Behavioral Science, the Institute of General Economic Research, and the Department of Empirical Economic Research and Econometrics, University of Freiburg i. Br.; Dr. Reto Müller, CEO and executive chair of the Helbling Group, Zurich; Siegmar Schulz, China manager of the Volkswagen factory (1986–2001) and manager of the Senior Experts' Service, Wolfsburg (since 2001); and Professor Bernd Schauenberg of the Faculty of Economic and Behavioral Science and the Institute of Economic Science, also director of the Business Management Institute III and chair of personal and organizational economics, University of Freiburg i. Br.

Contents

Note on transcription

The Pinyin transcription system is used throughout the book, except for a very few Chinese names that have alternative transcriptions traditionally used in the English-speaking world.

World Economic Summit 2050 in Shanghai

The Asiatic superpowers, including China, are holding discussions with America about new free-trade agreements. The Europeans are sitting at a side table. Germany, Britain, and France hope that protective tariffs will defend them against Asian imports. *The traditional economies have been economically relegated to the second division.*

(Joachim Althof, "Asien: Der unaufhaltsame Aufstieg" ["Asia: The inexorable rise"], *Finanz€n*, Munich, no. 4, April 1, 2004, pp. 26–7)

Perhaps

the Middle Kingdom* might be able to provide food for thought to help counter this pessimistic outlook. This book investigates a particular way of looking at things, a way of coping with a confused world. It originated centuries ago in China, but has barely even been heard of in the Western world. Presented in a compact form, it can help Western managers to gain a new—cunning—perspective on the old and the new, on the past and the future. It can breathe fresh life into the relatively stagnant, inward-looking European spirit that threatens European managers; it can broaden their perspective, hitherto clouded by a blind spot for recognizing ruses, and open their eyes to a "secret resource" that has never been rationally explained to them, so preventing them from being able to make full use of it! The economic advantages derived from China's geographical *location* may be pretty unattainable, but the advantages of the Chinese *standpoint*, derived, for example, from the cultivation of cunning, are within the reach of European managers, if they themselves also adopt this unconventional standpoint and equip their brains with additional—strategic—"software."

**Translators' note*: a historical term for China or its 18 inner provinces.

This is the reason

this book gives an introduction to the Chinese art of stratagem especially for Western managers. At the beginning of the book are three pictures. These depict what a "stratagem" or "ruse" is, and pictorialize a philosophical assumption that underlies the Chinese concept of cunning. Thereafter, the scope of the book extends from the general—the "16 Building Blocks of the Art of Stratagem"—to the specific—"Stratagem Training" for managers. In the general part, basic concepts are explained and misconceptions dispelled, as regards, for example, the relationship of Sun Tzu to the 36 stratagems, or of Machiavelli and Clausewitz to artifice. The crucial question in this context is introduced, a question that is never asked in Europe, but is often on the lips of the Chinese. The ethical dimension of the 36 stratagems is also examined. In the main part, which is devoted to stratagem training, Western managers are initiated into the offensive and defensive, the tactical and strategic practical application, as well as the inherent risks of the 36 stratagems.

As far as we know, this book is the first Western evaluation of Chinese works on the subject of the 36 stratagems in economics and management, which have been published by the score and command a large circulation in Taiwan and the People's Republic of China. It should help to overcome the great difference between Chinese and European executives in the technical skill of cunning, which is proving so damaging to Western economies.

The 36 Stratagems

According to the treatise *36 Stratagems: The Secret Book of the Art of War* (*Sanshiliu Ji: Miben Bingfa*) from circa AD 1500.

1. Crossing the sea while deceiving the heaven/Deceiving the emperor [by inviting him to a house by the sea that is really a disguised ship] and [thus causing him to] cross the sea
2. Besieging [the undefended capital of the country of] Wei to rescue Zhao [the country that has been attacked by the Wei forces]
3. Killing with a borrowed knife
4. Awaiting at one's ease the exhausted enemy
5. Taking advantage of a conflagration to commit robbery
6. Clamor in the east, attack in the west
7. Creating something out of nothing
8. Openly repairing the [burned wooden] walkway, in secret [before completing the repairs] marching to Chencang [to attack the enemy]
9. Observing the fire burning on the opposite shore [seemingly uninvolved]
10. Hiding the dagger behind a smile
11. Letting the plum tree wither in place of the peach tree
12. [Quick-wittedly] leading away the sheep [that unexpectedly crosses one's path]
13. Beating the grass to startle the snakes
14. Borrowing a corpse for the soul's return
15. Luring the tiger down from the mountain [onto the plain]
16. If one wishes to catch something, one has first to let it go
17. Tossing out a brick to attract jade
18. Catching the bandits by first catching the ringleader

19. Removing the firewood from under the cauldron
20. Clouding the water to catch the fish [robbed of their clear sight]
21. The cicada casts off its skin of gleaming gold
22. Shutting the door to capture the thief
23. Befriending a distant enemy to attack an enemy nearby
24. Borrowing a route [through the country of Yu] for an attack against [its neighboring country of] Guo [, in order to capture Yu after the conquest of Guo]
25. Stealing the beams and replacing the pillars [on the inside, while leaving the facade of the house unchanged]
26. Cursing the acacia, [while] pointing at the mulberry tree
27. Feigning madness without losing the balance
28. Removing the ladder after [the opponent] has climbed onto the roof
29. Decorating a [barren] tree with [artificial] flowers
30. Turning [the role of] the guest into [that of] the host
31. The stratagem of the beautiful man/woman
32. The stratagem of opening the gates [of a city that is unprepared for self-defense]
33. The special agent stratagem/The stratagem of sowing discord
34. The stratagem of the suffering flesh
35. The linking stratagem/Stratagem-linking
36. [When the situation is growing hopeless,] running away [in good time] is the best stratagem

By way of introduction, see *KdL*, *Strategeme 1*, *Strategeme 2*, and *List*; see also www.36strategeme.de

Pictures of Cunning

Diagram

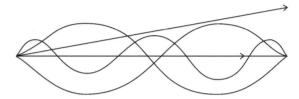

The straight line represents the uncontrived, hence "normal," conventional path from the starting point to the goal, or, as Carl von Clausewitz says, "the straight, simple, that is, direct way to behave."[1] The winding lines symbolize crafty, unconventional, nonroutine, stupefying, and, thus, cunning ways to the goal. The line leading to the other goal clearly shows the category of the escape stratagem.

Caricature

The caption to the drawing by Zheng Xinyao[2] reads: "Some 'cunning schemes' perpetrated by men seem to arise from the pressure that women exert on them."

How is the "cunning scheme"—namely, the ruse—represented in the drawing? With broom in hand, a wife waits for her husband until late into the night. She is clearly planning to welcome him with a good talking-to. Not being cunning herself, she only watches the normal route home. However, her husband has long since devised a cunning plan to get home using a different, unusual way, unobserved by his wife.

The caricature might also give managers something to think about. It may be that they look in only one direction—the direction in which one generally looks. But the cunning competitor has long since edged ahead via a completely different route. If, like the Chinese wife, you have a blind spot for recognizing cunning, you might only become aware of it when your cunning competitor has long since forged ahead. Cunning comes to the fore at unexpected times and in the most peculiar places. So you only see through it when you break away from conventional thinking. You will underestimate many things if you assume that somebody else's behavior always follows the same old plan.

Example

The following was written about a visit by Erwin Teufel, governor of Baden-Württemberg, to China in 1994:

> The Chinese are trying to encourage investment from Baden-Württemberg in an industrial area. A large tent is put up, and there is also a delegation from Singapore. Then something very embarrassing happens. Teufel is obliged to stand by as Japanese industrialists conclude a million-dollar contract. Group photo with the Japanese! The mayor says to Teufel, "That should encourage your businesses to conclude contracts here, too." (*B*, Stuttgart ed., April 26, 1994, p. 5)

Seen from the Chinese perspective, the Chinese behavior is not at all "embarrassing." Instead, the Chinese perceive it as a use of the provocation stratagem 13, "Beating the grass to startle the snakes."

The idea was to stimulate the German industrialists to enter into business with the Chinese as quickly and favorably as possible, spurred on by the fear that Japanese and Singaporean competition might snatch everything away from in front of their eyes.

The example shows that the Western pattern of thought alone is not enough if one wants to fully understand the non-Western world, in particular the Far East, and to handle it appropriately. So it is important to build and incorporate Chinese "cunning software" into the Western pattern of thought, and also to learn to analyze situations from the point of view of the Chinese art of stratagem. Because if you just build on Western ideas and "rationality," you will be left standing there helpless and confused, just like the wife in the caricature when confronted with cunning, be it in China or within our own cultural environment. Anyone who thinks that globalization just means the international passage of money and goods, but not the exchange of knowledge from West to East and vice versa, is unlikely to have a bright future ahead of them; the same applies to anyone whose concept of globalization does not include the expansion of their own horizons through the acquisition of non-Western know-how, for example, knowledge of stratagems.

Philosophical design of cunning

According to the ancient Chinese yin-yang symbol representing the world, first, the bright yang (right) cannot exist without the dark yin (left), and second, in the middle of yang, so in the middle of the symbol for light, there is a dark yin point. Yang and yin are dependent on each other. If one element were to be removed, the other element would perish. Yang symbolizes the sky, the sun, man, and light, hence lack of cunning. Yin stands for the earth, the moon, woman, and darkness, hence cunning. According to the oldest Chinese oracle classic, the Book of Changes (first half of the first millennium BC), yang has the number 9 and yin the number 6, so 36 appears as the square of the yin element, and therefore as the symbol for a great deal of cunning. This might be the reason why the Chinese used the number 36 for listing different stratagem techniques. In the West, the "central metaphor of the Enlightenment is light" (*Der Spiegel*, no. 33, 2001, p. 175), which is why the Enlightenment (in French *les Lumières*, literally "the lights") pushed the darkness, the supposedly irrational, and therefore also cunning, into the background. The West is proud of the Enlightenment and regards it as one of the most important achievements of the occidental mind. Of course, there are also anti-Enlightenment trends in the West, such as the German Romantics, who are more receptive to darkness and the underground. But, with its quest for light and clarity, and its conquering of darkness, the Enlightenment predominates, particularly in modern Western thinking. No wonder that in the Enlightenment opera *The Magic Flute* the Queen of the Night represents evil—and that the very first sentence of the opera mentions cunning in a negative sense: "Help, help, otherwise I am lost, chosen as an offering to the cunning snake." Ideas such as "The bringer of light need not fear the darkness" (*NZZ*, March 17, p. 45) are not widespread. The Enlightenment way of thinking, whereby human reason functions largely without cunning, can be traced back to Plato with his eternal world of ideas (*Strategeme 2*, pp. 27ff.; *KdL*, pp. 38ff.).

The unbalanced turning towards the light, which at least in part characterizes Western thought, must seem one-sided to the Chinese with their yin-yang symbolism, whereby light and shadow are mutually dependent and complement one another. Even in the yang element, which symbolizes light, there is, as already mentioned, a dark point. It shows that even in the brightest light, and so not just at nighttime but also in plain daylight, cunning is to be expected. In the same way, a white point shines in the yin part, the symbol of darkness. So the blackness is not absolute: meaning basically that every ruse has a snag.

16 Building Blocks of the Art of Stratagem

Stratagem and cunning

"Stratagem" is a word meaning a "ruse of war," and an "artifice" or "trick" in general. The word "cunning" often has a negative slant. For this reason, I prefer the relatively unknown neutral word "stratagem." Because, in the Chinese language, words for "cunning," notably *zhi*, have a neutral or even positive slant. I will go into this in greater detail in the section on "Stratagem and wisdom."

The word "stratagem" has two meanings here. First, a specific trick technique, such as one directed at making something (a company balance sheet, for instance) appear much more attractive than it actually is. Second, "stratagem" denotes the linguistic description of this technique. The Chinese coined the phrase "Decorating a [barren] tree with [artificial] flowers" to describe the trick of making something appear more attractive than it actually is. I also use "stratagem," or sometimes "stratagem phrase," as a *designation* for this and other ruses. So the expression "36 stratagems" describes two different things: First, 36 trick techniques, that is, modus operandi, and second, 36 designations of trick techniques, that is, 36 stratagem phrases that verbalize the various trick techniques in an easily remembered and concise form.

Stratagem and blindness to cunning

When confronted with an unusual occurrence, alarm bells ring for Chinese people who know the 36 stratagems or even just a few of them. Familiar with stratagems from an early age through popular tales of trickery, they assign the incident, often instinctively, to a stratagem. They suspect a trick even when none may be intended. But this extreme sensitivity to cunning, characteristic of much of the Chinese population, particularly those in management positions, acts like a protective shield. In nine out of ten cases, the suspicion of a trick might prove unfounded, but in the tenth case it might protect the subject from harm.

Blindness to trickery denotes an inability to recognize a trick, whether it is or has been used by an opponent, between third parties, observed from outside, or even in one's own spontaneous crafty behavior or reactions. Blindness to cunning leads to an inability to work with cunning. Even a person who has a blind spot for recognizing ruses will use a trick here or there, but probably unknowingly, spontaneously, without recognizing its cunning nature. This means that in many instances one's own use of tricks will be accordingly dubious and poor (see *KdL*, pp. 142ff.). This is where the Chinese art of stratagem can help. For "models and theories have their place; without them everything would be much harder—the highly rated intuition alone is barely enough for sustainable success" (*HandelsZeitung*, Zurich, March 10, 2004, p. 15). Often people who have a blind spot for cunning will miss out on an opportunity to use a helpful, ethically sound trick because they don't have an arsenal of tricks up their sleeve. Jesus Christ's advice was "Be as shrewd as snakes and as innocent as doves." In this little-known biblical saying, "shrewdness" can be understood as the ability to see through and, when possible, foil destructive tricks. So it would seem that awareness of cunning certainly fits into the Christian ethos. Jesus himself demonstrated this awareness of cunning when he saw through and foiled Satan's wiles to tempt him in the desert. Unfortunately, the admonition to be as shrewd as snakes fell on deaf ears in the Western world. But another civilization can offer a good antidote to blindness to trickery: the 36 stratagems from the Middle Kingdom.

Stratagems and the art and knowledge of stratagem

The Chinese art of cunning is not just restricted to 36 pithy phrases, that is, 36 expressions of trick techniques, but is based on an examination of the ruses of war in military theoretical works that goes back thousands of years, and on a veritable bible of tactics (see www.36strategeme.de, "Traktat" ["Treatise"]). It is also based on specialist literature on the 36 stratagems, comprising hundreds of works, that has recently flourished in China. There is no need for Westerners slavishly to adopt the Chinese "art of stratagem," but they can build on it, in line with a quotation from Johann Gottfried von Herder (1744–1803):

> Let us learn what we can learn, because it is already there, others have invented it for us. Let us add what we can add, so that we may also take our place with dignity, and leave behind more … than we have received.[3]

So, in this book, I do not just translate Chinese texts on management and stratagems, but also present some of my own insights based on the Chinese art of stratagem.

I see the "knowledge of stratagem" as being the ability, gained through the study of the art of stratagem, to handle cunning effectively, whether through the offensive use of cunning, or through the defensive unveiling of cunning. Knowledge of stratagem is therefore the rationally structured "ability to deviate from the routine," oriented towards problem-solving and based on cunning. Of course, as a manager, particularly when dealing with China, it is important not to neglect the completely normal, conventional methods of problem-solving. I am not an advocate of "panstratagemism," whereby each and every thing might only be analyzed and resolved by means of stratagems. Certainly, it can be advisable to view even "quite normal" happenings, which appear completely free of trickery, from the stratagem perspective, in order to uncover, just in time, a trick which is concealed precisely in such "quite normal" happenings. But although it is important to exercise vigilance and caution, one should avoid becoming preoccupied with stratagems to the detriment of "conventional knowledge," for example, legal considerations, as well as the rules of etiquette and propriety. "Conventional knowledge" is—according to the yin-yang symbol—crucial for one half of reality, with this half providing the fundamental basis for problem-solving.

To quote an example: The German company Diehl had its name translated into Chinese and printed on its managers' business cards. It seems that the native Chinese translator confused the German *ie* with an *ei*, as in *Osterei* (Easter egg). He translated *Diehl* as *Dai'ao*.[4] The Chinese character *dai* means "acting on behalf of," and the character *ao* means "arrogance." So, in Chinese, the company name translated into "arrogantly acting on behalf of," obviously to the detriment of the company's image.

This example shows how important it is to handle with care "ordinary" matters that have nothing to do with trickery, both in general and in business dealings with the Chinese. In a situation like this, it is vital to employ the services of a sinological expert who speaks your language, for the purposes of language-checking. Being a manager should always mean drawing on all sources of knowledge and making a profit out of it.

Stratagem and strategy

These two words are frequently confused. "Stratagem" is another word for "ruse," or "artifice." By "strategy" managers usually understand "long-term planning with regard to basic company targets," as opposed to "tactics" in the sense of "short-term planning." Long-term plans—strategies—and likewise short-term plans—tactics—can be completely free of cunning. For this reason, one should differentiate between a stratagem, a strategy, and a tactic.

A stratagem may be used strategically, that is, with a long-term objective relevant to the basic company targets, but also tactically, that is, short-term, as well as operatively, involving the overarching planning of several tactical steps. A distinction must therefore be made between a strategic, operative, and tactical use of stratagem.

Stratagem and deception

Stratagem is a neutral word for "trickery" or "cunning." So an explanation must be given of what a "trick" is. Trickery is often equated with deception. But it is important to get away from this narrow definition of trickery. The best Chinese description of a "trick" is "Create something unusual to achieve a victory" (*Chu qi zhi sheng*). This saying corresponds to the *Duden** definition of a trick: "a means by which one (by deceiving others) tries to achieve something that could not be achieved by normal means." *Duden* puts "deceiving others" in parentheses because deception is not essential for trickery. So there is also a form of trickery that is free of deception. In short, trickery is an artful, unusual, cunning means of solving problems, which sometimes—but by no means always—entails the use of deception.

The *Duden* definition of the trick is, unfortunately, largely unknown. Most people's knowledge of cunning is generally shaped by the idea that cunning is another word for deception. This is the reason why we initially have problems with the Chinese concept of trickery, because it interprets trickery very broadly and extends to a variety of behaviors; it even classifies as "trickery" behaviors judged not to be trickery by someone who would generally consider trickery to be deception. If you don't want to be taken in by behaviors that you don't suspect of cunning, then you need to engage with and adopt the broad Chinese concept of trickery.

**Translators' note*: Dudenverlag is the publisher of the definitive German dictionary, which is commonly referred to as *Duden*.

Stratagem and lie

As far as I know, cunning has never been defined by a Western philosopher, unlike the lie, which was defined centuries ago. As long ago as the fourth century, Augustine (354–430)—if one can call him a philosopher—explained what a lie is, namely, "a false statement born from the desire to deceive."[5] Later, other thinkers added two further elements: First, that the person on the receiving end really is given the wrong idea, and second, that this person is entitled to the truth.

In current German-speaking literature, there is a whole plethora of books with the word "lie" in the title. But works containing the word "cunning" in the title are thin on the ground. The aim of the lie is always to deceive, whether by making something up or concealing something. So it comes into the category of deception stratagems, and is essentially already covered by one particular stratagem, namely, stratagem 7, "Creating something out of nothing" (simulation) or—turned around—"Creating nothing out of something" (dissimulation or concealment). If one spends too much time worrying about lies, which are just one small part of the art of stratagem, one runs the danger of overlooking the broad arsenal of artifices that are free from lies and deception, and of remaining unaware of this aspect of cunning.

Stratagem and wisdom

If you strike on an unconventional solution to a problem that surprises an opponent, the Chinese perceive this as a sign of cleverness and resourcefulness. So it is no surprise that the main Chinese character for "wisdom" and "intelligence," among others denoting a Confucian cardinal virtue, namely,

(zhi),

also means "stratagem." Knowledge of stratagem, thus, appears as a sign of intelligence. The wise person might or, rather, ought to be familiar with tricks, and in particular to be able to see through them—and is admired for that.

Blindness to cunning is seen as stupidity and is ridiculed. Of course, the intelligence of the cunning person is always relative. Compared to someone who is even stupider, a stupid person may be a little bit cleverer and capable of outsmarting them with his "small intelligence" (*xiao congming*).

Even in a case like this, the stratagem user is slightly more intelligent than the victim of the trick. If one is aware that the Chinese view cunning as a shrewd and unconventional way to solve a problem, it comes as no surprise that they admire cunning as an outlet for creativity and intelligence. The Chinese perceive the ruse as a product of wisdom, of the intellect. For the Chinese with their concept of *sapientia* (wisdom), *Homo sapiens* is always also a *Homo dolosus* (cunning man). Quite different in the Western world—for instance, the British philosopher of the Enlightenment John Locke wrote that cunning is merely the ape of wisdom. It is similar to wisdom, but as fundamentally different from wisdom as the ape is from mankind. It is true that in ancient Hellas, wisdom (*mêtis*) also had a crafty element to it, but "nowhere in Greece do we come across a theory about it" (Jullien, p. 22). Even the German word *List* (cunning) used to mean "wisdom" in times gone by. But those were just episodes in the history of the Western concept of wisdom. In the Middle Kingdom, the character shown above has retained the dual meaning of "wisdom" and "stratagem" throughout the millennia.

So the Chinese have been cultivating cunning for an eternity. At least during the Christian era, Westerners trivialized, condemned, or ignored trickery. In light of this, it is not surprising that it was not Europeans, but Chinese who put together the only (as far as we know) list of ruses in the world—the 36 stratagems.

Stratagem and economics

In 2004, at my instigation, the Faculty of Economics at the Albert-Ludwig University of Freiburg (Germany) held the interdisciplinary seminar "Cunning in business" for the fourth time in a row. This seminar arouses great interest in prospective business economists, who also include some future managers. A result of the seminars held to date has been the realization that cunning is not considered a subject for research in economics. Despite the fact that business obviously provides the ideal seedbed for the use of stratagems, because of the numerous information asymmetries, target divergences, and power differentials among the economic players; because of the extent of economic events of which it is becoming increasingly difficult to gain an overview in this age of globalization—this "anarchy of global order, which is actually disorder" (*Die Zeit*, November 8, 2001, p. 43); and because of the powerful role of the psychology of the economic players, which is so open to manipulation with tricks.

One of the economics lecturers involved thought that the stratagem perspective could be used to gain a different understanding of various economic phenomena and to classify numerous economic manifestations according to other organizational criteria.

I couldn't help but think that economics is frantically trying to sweep cunning under the carpet. For instance, the prevailing mainstream economic theory about *Homo oeconomicus* (economic man) is that he is a self-interested individual, who acts to obtain the highest possible well-being for himself, and who behaves in a strictly rational manner. During one of the "Cunning in business" seminars, my question about the content of this strictly rational behavior received the reply that cunning behavior doesn't come into it. Certain specialist terms used in economics also seem determined to push cunning out of sight. For example, postcontractual so-called opportunistic behavior is termed a "*moral* hazard." By way of illustration, it might be that in a relationship between a boss and an employee, the employee does not communicate new knowledge or conveys it in such a way that the boss draws the wrong conclusions. Behavior like this is termed "opportunistic" by economists. In my opinion, using the term "opportunistic" diverts attention away from the cunning nature of the episode. Instead of relegating the incident to the realms of ethics and speaking of "moral hazard," it would be more clear-sighted to talk of "stratagemic" hazard and more appropriate to speak of "cunning" than "opportunism."

Stratagem and "economic warfare"

In mainland China and Taiwan, managers are presented with numerous stratagem books. They are based on the Chinese tendency to compare the "marketplace" with a "war place" (*shangchang ru zhanchang*). Admittedly, this opinion is not universally championed.

> The 36 stratagems are a military philosophy handed down to us by our ancestors as a cultural inheritance. Their main purpose is to get the better of a military enemy. But the people we are dealing with today are colleagues who deserve to be treated with respect and solicitousness. For this reason, we should not label commerce as "economic warfare." In the framework of economic competition, both sides should win. The basic tenet of our relationship with our fellow men and women should be to "help instead of fight each other," and the guiding principle in trade should be commercial virtue. ("The 36 stratagems questioned," *New People's Evening News*, Shanghai, May 19, 2002, p. 13; see also *Strategeme 2*, pp. 20ff.)

Despite warnings such as this, the general assumption in China is that the wisdom that accompanies a general into battle is the same that guides the executive in the world of business. This is an idea that has prevailed in China for more than 2,000 years. There are more than 80 books dealing with the subject of the 36 stratagems and economic warfare in one form or another. Admittedly, they do stand side by side with books that have less warlike titles, such as *The 36 Stratagems and Business Management* (Chen 1). As far as I know, none of these books has been translated into a Western language. In these books, there is an unmistakable tendency for economic matters to be viewed from a military perspective, exemplified, for instance, by the customer being portrayed as the "enemy" that has to be "conquered." This viewpoint extends beyond China to other countries, such as Singapore, Japan, Vietnam, and Korea, where the 36 stratagems are equally well known.

"They behave as if it were war," say Westerners, and not just about Chinese competitors (*Der Spiegel*, no. 50, 2002, p. 150). In the West too, you hear sentences such as—from the mouth of a manager in Zurich—"war rules" in the world of business (*Das Magazin*, weekend supplement of the *TA*, no. 8, 2004, p. 22). In Paris, there is even a "School of Economic Warfare" (*HBM*, November 2003, pp. 74ff.). Terms such as "price war" are not uncommon in the Western world and—just like in the Middle Kingdom—are not always meant as dramatically as they sound. In any case, when you view management and economics from a stratagemic point of view, you do occasionally have to adopt a certain warlike perspective on business life.

Stratagem and manager

Similar to "strategy," the word "manager" is used in an inflated way, with even Jesus being described as a manager.[6] Nowadays, when a cleaner assumes the title of "waste-management manager," an assistant bookkeeper that of "finance manager," a bartender that of "restaurant manager," and a caretaker that of "facility manager," this use of the word does, of course, contain a stratagemic element (stratagem 29: "Decorating a [barren] tree with [artificial] flowers"). In today's world, all possible spheres of activity are dignified by the addendum "management," from "quality management" and "water management" to—for managers in danger of burnout— "health management." Numerous fashionable management concepts that are conveyed using specialist terms such as "customer-relationship management" may sometimes promise more than they deliver. Management exists not just in industry, but also under the name of "new public management" in government administration. Politicians are expected to have managerial qualities; hence, they might be reproached for their "poor management." It is certainly no compliment when a politician is said to be "regarded as no more than a manager, technocrat, pen-pusher, and manipulator" (*NZZ*, February 7/8, 2004, p. 3). But "management qualities are essential" not just for businesspeople and politicians, but also for mothers (*NZZ*, November 21, 2000, p. B. 3).

"Managers analyze, plan, calculate, allocate resources, and monitor the achievement of goals. They introduce management systems, organize processes by which things should be done, coordinate different areas of responsibility, and establish order and routine. They are in fact really optimizing technocrats who orient their behavior according to numbers and act fully in the spirit of Peter Drucker's saying, 'What gets measured gets managed.'" As managers, they recognize and create "a line of approach, generate great trust, and effect an atmosphere of change without creating a sense of yearning for the past. They practice what they preach" (*NZZ*, November 21, 2000, p. B. 1).

Recently, however, this idealized picture has ceased to reflect many managers. "Many managers have discredited themselves through amateurish behavior. Even more damaging has been a noticeable decline in decency and moral standards ... Greed and a certain detachment from reality seem to have encouraged some managers to indulge in the unscrupulous pursuit of money, sometimes only barely on this side of the borders of legality, and sometimes even on the other side. By using underhand tricks and deliberately misleading the public, from stockholders to the authorities, the breach of confidence has reached new heights" (*NZZ*, July 13/14, 2002, p. 19).

Numerous management methods that do not involve the use of cunning at all have been devised in the West. These management techniques facilitate system integration and the optimization of all business processes, resulting in clear structures and ordered procedures, as well as boosting initiative and innovation, particularly at middle-management level, and this is one of the elements of Western civilization that the inhabitants of the People's Republic of China are studying assiduously with the aim of introducing it into the Middle Kingdom. "We want to create new products by importing assets and know-how, advanced techniques, and *modern management*," says Zhang Lichang, for example, a member of the 25-strong politburo of China's Communist Party and party leader of the trade and industry town of Tianjin (*Der Spiegel*, no. 17, 2004, p. 115). But this does not stop the Chinese from having themselves instructed in the application of the 36 stratagems to management at the same time. This is all about linking together conventional methods (in this instance, Western management concepts) with cunning behaviors derived from unconventional patterns of thought, which are crystallized in the 36 stratagems. This combination of conventional and unconventional approaches was already being advocated 2,500 years ago in the oldest military treatise in the world (Master Sun's *The Art of War*). From the Chinese point of view (Li, p. 3), both Western management know-how and Chinese stratagem skills are indispensable. Beyond sheer motivation to achieve, perseverance, and determination, this sort of combination can also help Western managers become more agile-minded, and encourage their multidimensional and associative awareness; of course, they must always act within the boundaries of ethical behavior.

In specialist books, there is frequently little differentiation made between the words "manager" and "leader." After all, the English verb "to manage" means, among other things, "to lead" or "to guide." In this book, "manager" should be understood in a broad sense, that of a generally employed, though in some cases self-employed, leader, namely, a person in a position of authority within a hierarchical organizational structure, who carries out managerial duties at completely different levels of the hierarchy, not just in a business environment, but also in other areas. Managers are bound up in a multifaceted web of life, and so come into contact with lots of different stratagemic situations, not just the intrigues of business life. For this reason, it would be wrong to interpret the subject of 36 stratagems for business too narrowly. In any case, it is important, particularly for managers who work at an international level, to have not just money, but also stratagem skills, at their disposal. Because it can prove beneficial to those market players who don't just constantly wheel out and try to use the old familiar maxims, but who think unconventionally, question rules, and utilize the power of their own creativity, thus creating advantages in innovation and business.

The 36 stratagems and Master Sun (Sun Tzu)

"Make a noise in the east, attack in the west," "Lure the tiger down from the mountains," "Conceal the dagger with the smile," and "Wait relaxed for the worn out"—these four stratagems from the catalog of 36 stratagems, translated in several instances rather clumsily, appeared in a special supplement to the *Financial Times Deutschland* (*FTD*) about the People's Republic of China. The source of each of the four stratagems is quoted as "Master Sun." In an explanatory note, the renowned newspaper writes: "Master Sun is known to posterity because of a book attributed to him that is read by many managers today: 'The Art of War'" (*FTD*, November 28, 2003, p. 32).

Three of the four stratagems published by the *FTD* do not originate from Master Sun (see in detail *KdL*, pp. 57, 60, 63). The only saying that can be traced back to Master Sun is "Awaiting at one's ease the exhausted enemy" (translated inaccurately by the *FTD* as "Wait relaxed for the worn out"). It is number 4 in the list of the 36 stratagems. The mistake made by the *FTD* is not uncommon. For instance, in an American managers' book published in 2003, the 36 stratagems are again linked to Master Sun, about whom it is said: "it is most likely that [he] was aware of the 36 stratagems."[7] So there is some confusion surrounding Master Sun and the 36 stratagems. Master Sun, thought to be a contemporary of Confucius (551–479 BC), actually formulated just one of the 36 stratagems, namely, the one cited above. The other 35 stratagems were formulated by other Chinese in completely different centuries, most of them a long time after Master Sun.

The book *The Art of War* introduces the fundamental terms and the seeds of the Chinese art of stratagem, which was only developed later (see *KdL*, pp. 46ff.). *The Art of War* lists "12 cunning ways" (*Strategeme 2*, pp. 47ff.). If one compares the wording of the 12 cunning ways with that of the 36 stratagems, there is just one single concurrence. The Chinese wording of the eleventh cunning way is roughly equivalent to that of stratagem 4, "Awaiting at one's ease the exhausted enemy." Some of the 12 listed ways are also recognizably related in spirit to some stratagems in the catalog of the 36 stratagems.

Even if Master Sun's 12 cunning ways may have influenced the content of the 36 stratagems, this does not mean to say that Master Sun formulated the 36 stratagems. There is a yawning time lapse of at least two millennia between Master Sun's work and the 36 stratagems. *The Art of War* deals with the whole issue of waging war, including the conventional non-cunning as well as the unconventional cunning. So it is true to say that Master Sun created the basis of the Chinese art of stratagem. However, the treatment of cunning was just one issue for Master Sun. The catalog of the 36 stratagems takes up this particular aspect of *The Art of War*. Presented in a condensed form, this "database of cunning" conveys the Chinese art of stratagem at a much more highly developed level than that of Master Sun, and is enriched by the wealth of experience in cunning gathered over the 20 centuries since Master Sun's death.

A question never posed in Europe, but frequently raised in China

The difference in perception of cunning between Europeans and Chinese can be clearly seen in quotations from Machiavelli's most famous work *The Prince* and one of China's best-known folk tales *Journey to the West*. Machiavelli (1469–1527), whose name springs instinctively to the lips of Western managers whenever they hear the word "cunning," uses the words "cunning" or "trick" several times in his work *The Prince*, but never actually names a specific technique. He only describes individual crafty behaviors, recounting cunning anecdotes.

For instance, he writes that Cesare Borgia "resorted to cunning" (*The Prince*, Chapter 7). But then he simply describes what happened: "He knew so well how to conceal his mind that … the Orsini were reconciled, so that their simplicity brought them into his power at Sinigaglia," where he had them murdered (see *Strategeme 2*, pp. 275–6).[8]

A passage like this, where the author speaks explicitly of "cunning," is the highest level of awareness of cunning to be found in Western literary or scientific works for close on three millennia, since ancient Hellas. Machiavelli does not name the trick that Cesare Borgia uses. But anyone familiar with the catalog of the 36 stratagems can immediately identify Borgia's trick. He used stratagem 10, "Hiding the dagger behind a smile." Had the victims of Cesare Borgia's trick been familiar with the catalog of the 36 stratagems, they might have been more alert to Borgia's lethal charm offensive and might not have been so naively taken in by his cunning.

The awareness of cunning in the book *Journey to the West*, from the time of the Ming dynasty (1368–1644), appears one level higher than in Machiavelli, and is representative of the accuracy with which the Chinese recognize cunning. At one point, the Monkey King fights a monster. Vanquished, the latter flees the battle arena. The Monkey King and his companion, the pig monk, stay hard on his heels. The monster is at its wits' end. The following is an original quotation from the novel *Journey to the West*:

> The monster resorted to the stratagem *The cicada casts off its skin of gleaming gold*. It rolled on the ground and reassumed its original tiger form ... The monster saw its pursuers hurrying ever closer. It struck a hole in its chest fur and tore off the fur. Then it cast the skin over a large rock and changed into a violent gust of wind ... When the monster later gave a report to his master, the King of the Yellow Wind, it was keen to point out: "Just as they were chasing me and tried to attack me, I used the stratagem *The cicada casts off its skin of gleaming gold*" ... The Monkey King and pig monk had seen the tiger fall and flop down outstretched onto a rock. The Monkey King raised his iron bar up into the air and brought it down with all his might, but it simply bounced back up off the hard stone ... Likewise the pig monk hit out with his rake, but its prongs also rebounded. It was only then that they realized that it was just a tiger's fur that they had struck ... Greatly startled, the Monkey King cried out: "No, no! We have fallen for its stratagem!"—"What stratagem?" asked the pig monk.—"It goes, *The cicada casts off its skin of gleaming gold*. The monster left the tiger's skin covering this rock and made a leisurely escape."[9]

This is not just the portrayal of a cunning incident. Over and above that, the writer, the victim of the trick, and its perpetrator all identify the trick technique used, which corresponds to the stratagem wording that is listed as number 21 in the catalog of the 36 stratagems. Nowhere in the whole of Western literature, including modern management literature, is such a high degree of specialized knowledge of cunning documented. Since Europe first came into being, a European has never asked the question "What stratagem?" either in a novel or in real life. This is a question that Europeans cannot ask, because they do not have the terminology for the various trick techniques.

Something that is missing from language will also be missing from thought. Because of the lack of suitable terminology for cunning, a European is unable to think about tricks rationally and communicate competently about them. As far as Europeans are concerned, every trick is a new one. No wonder that the Prussian King Frederick the Great (1712–1786) said, "The number of stratagems is never-ending" (Larousse, p. 1132).

Carl von Clausewitz's view of cunning: five prejudices challenged

Western prejudices about cunning are condensed into a very concise form in a remark by the Prussian military theorist Carl von Clausewitz (1780–1831):

> The weaker the powers of the strategic leader become, the more open he will be to cunning, so that *cunning* presents itself *as a last resort* to *the very weak and small*, for whom *caution and wisdom no longer suffice*, to the point where all skill appears to have deserted him. The more helpless his position, the more everything becomes concentrated into one single desperate blow, and the more willingly cunning comes to the side of his boldness.[10]

Five prejudices are reflected in these words.

1. Clausewitz does not give a moment's thought to the recognition of an enemy's cunning, which for him is only the emergency measure of a "very weak" opponent, hence something insignificant. There is no need to see through cunning, it is just there to be used—at the last minute.

2. According to Clausewitz, the combination of "power + cunning" does not exist. This lays the foundations for a twofold blindness to cunning.

    a. You are not prepared for cunning to be used by a powerful opponent, for example, a global corporation, and merely expect a straightforward and highly transparent display of power.

    b. If you are powerful yourself, you will waste no unnecessary thought on the use of cunning and just flex your muscles (which can prove very uneconomical).

3. Clausewitz believes that cunning only comes into play when wisdom is exhausted. He separates cunning from wisdom and intelligence. So where does cunning come from? Apparently from the gut; it is merely the chance result of spontaneous intuitive inspiration.

4. Clausewitz perceives cunning to have nothing to do with caution. Carefully considered, well-thought-out cunning calculation is apparently completely alien to him. He sees cunning as a product of daring recklessness. The gambler acts cunningly. By holding this opinion, Clausewitz encourages a purely instinctive amateurish use of cunning, which is so typical for Europeans and proves damaging to them over and over again.

5. As Clausewitz treats cunning simply as "a last resort," it seems that his perception of it as a tactical method is restricted to its use as a last-minute means of salvation. By taking this attitude, Clausewitz precludes any discussion about the strategic application of cunning.

It's not surprising that cunning appears to play no part in Western management literature. For example, in the monumental work *Campus Management* (two volumes, Frankfurt/New York 2003, 2,160 pages [originally published in English under the title *Business,*

Bloomsbury Publishing Plc, 2002]), the keyword "cunning" is not listed in the subject index, although it does make an occasional appearance in the text—merely in passing. Successful management without any cunning is suggested by Stuart Crainer's book *The 75 Greatest Management Decisions Ever Made* (New York 1999). Words such as cunning or trick are not mentioned at all, but "shrewdness" does get a look-in just once—in a negative context. In the standard management books written in the West that relate to the Middle Kingdom, there is generally no mention of stratagems. Two American authors cite "Eight Elements" that should be taken into account when dealing with the Chinese, namely, personal connections (*guanxi*), the intermediary, social status, interpersonal harmony, holistic thinking, thrift, face, and endurance. No reference is made to the Chinese knowledge of stratagem, despite one or another application of a stratagem being described, albeit referred to as a "tactic" (*HBR*, October 2003, pp. 82ff.).

Cunning is not treated with such disdain in the Middle Kingdom. "The Chinese emphasize stratagems, Westerners emphasize force," declares Xue Guo'an rather succinctly in his book *A Comparative Study of "Master Sun's Art of War" and* [Clausewitz's] *"On War"*.[11] Anyone wishing to do something towards resolving this conflict has to formulate the exact opposite standpoint to each of the five prejudices that Clausewitz expresses about cunning. Then you might get close to the Chinese concept of cunning. Perhaps Clausewitz's opinion on cunning could be rewritten like this: "Weak as well as strong powers are open to cunning, which, being a dangerous weapon, should, whenever possible, be used with the greatest caution and wisdom, by carefully selecting the best cunning technique for the particular context. It may be used for any tactical or strategic purposes. Basically, cunning is available in any situation as an alternative route to a goal. Constant analysis of the potential use of cunning by the enemy is imperative to survival."

36 Chinese stratagems and their practical application in the West

Most of the cunning behaviors advocated by the 36 stratagems were, and still are, used outside China as well. However, they are generally used spontaneously, in an unconsidered way, and without the benefit of there being a linguistic tag to name the cunning behavior, as is the case with the catalog of the 36 stratagems. As a result of a lack of awareness of cunning, tricks generally remain unnoticed and unanalyzed.

A benefit that Western managers can draw from the catalog of the 36 stratagems is overcoming a blind spot for recognizing trickery. Eve apparently fell victim to it against the snake, as did Europa, daughter of the king of Phoenicia, after whom the continent of Europe was named, against the god Zeus, who first lured her away from her home by transforming himself into a bull, and then seduced her (see *Strategeme 2*, 35.11: Die genasführte Europa [The tricking of Europa]). It appears from these legends that blindness to cunning has been an ingrained characteristic of Europeans since the very beginning of time.

The Chinese art of stratagem, with the catalog of the 36 stratagems at its heart, provides managers with a truly *comprehensive vocabulary of cunning*. The individual stratagem techniques are often paraphrased with metaphors—open to narrow or broad interpretation—which do take a certain amount of getting used to. But that shouldn't prove too difficult: After all, Western priests use biblical stories allegorically to interpret current events.

An eye-opener to Western managers, the catalog of the 36 stratagems gives them a hitherto unavailable *overview* of the resource of cunning as an unconventional additional means to achieve goals. General access to the resource of cunning also provides a universal insight into a variety of possible types of destructive cunning behavior, and creates the conditions for seeing through it relatively comprehensively and for frustrating it in time. It is this stratagem *prevention*, this prevention of the damage that can result from the use of cunning, that is particularly important to managers.

Reality only assumes value if it is interpreted. The framework of the 36 stratagems provides one opportunity to interpret and structure reality.

At the end of 2003, a book was published in China in which the author analyzed the success of the computer company Cisco from the point of view of the 36 stratagems.[12] This shows how the 36 stratagems combined with the associated specialized terminology form a cognitive analytical web that the Chinese cast over reality— be it Chinese or foreign—in order to identify its cunning elements, interpret it from a stratagemic point of view, and use the result, that is, stratagem-based information, as a compass for utilizing this reality.

What you acquire in particular from the art of stratagem is a fairly comprehensive cunning *perspective* on life, which is new to the West. It enables you to have a focused view of the world. It can be compared to a new kind of *spotlight* that illuminates apparently familiar objects in a different way, highlighting things that up until now have remained unnoticed, or making aspects that have always seemed to act in isolation appear for the first time in a coherent light or an unexpected context.

Bremen professor of psychology Ulrich Kühnen is right when he says, "Westerners can, to a certain extent, pretty much learn to think like Asians" (*NZZ am Sonntag*, March 28, 2004, p. 76). The comprehensive Chinese stratagemic vision of reality is, of course, unfamiliar to Europeans, who tend to perceive ruses selectively and instinctively. But Europeans can acquire this rationale of comprehensive astuteness without too much effort, especially as they use cunning no less frequently than the Chinese, but without being fully aware of it. Europeans *practice* cunning unashamedly, but are ashamed to *speak* of it. As it doesn't come from Europe, the Chinese art of stratagem provides a non-Western "other ... frame of reference," an "external point of view" (François Jullien, *24 Heures*, Geneva, May 2, 1996, p. 48). Thanks to this, Europeans can for once view reality not from a Western angle, but from an outside perspective, and possibly even discover new facets of it, which they can then put to their own use.

Ruses are used in every human society, including in the West. You don't need to know the 36 stratagems to use them. But if you do know the 36 stratagems, you can use ruses more methodically and responsibly, and optimize their use. There's no longer any need to rely on spontaneous intuition, to listen to "gut feelings," because whenever you need to, you can just select the most suitable trick from a whole arsenal of stratagems. Taking into account a wealth of precedents associated with the cunning technique in question, you can plan your own cunning course of action and calculate the potential side effects. The list of the 36 stratagems will also enable you to scrutinize the behavior of opponents based on possible or presumed stratagems, and make sure you are well prepared in good time for them. And finally, before making a move, you can use the checklist of the 36 stratagems to analyze your own behavior from the point of view of stratagem prevention, and ask yourself the question: How can I structure my actions so that my opponent cannot use them in a stratagemic way?

The 36 stratagems equip Europeans with an aid to interpretation, enabling them to understand the artful behavior in a coherent manner. Behavior that, were it not for this way of viewing things, they would inaccurately label as cynicism or manipulation, or not even pay attention to, they can instead place in a broad, comprehensive context due to the stratagemic point of view.

Using the Chinese art of stratagem, Europeans can put their own Western—imperfect—views of cunning on a non-European basis, thus not just broadening them but also putting them into perspective; because a background that also draws on Chinese knowledge will naturally be broader than a background based exclusively on European culture. Learning the 36 stratagems puts Europeans into a position where they can rise above the ruse as a mere anecdote, make sense of a series of seemingly unrelated incidences of cunning, and, instead, reduce the countless bits of detailed information to just a few baselines. This does not, however, result in the simplification of the complexities of reality. It is rather a case of Westerners having their eyes opened to a complex reality, when they find their blind spot for recognizing trickery healed. In addition, they can learn to master stratagemic logic and rationality, guided by cunning to complement their current conventional logic, namely, rationality that is blind to cunning.

Admittedly, without making the effort to think for oneself, it is impossible to pluck out obvious solutions for individual cases from the list of 36 stratagems. The 36 stratagems are not a "cookbook" with recipes to be followed to the letter. The 36 stratagems just point out possible cunning directions and provide unconventional food for thought. They raise awareness of the use of cunning, which in Europe has, up until now, been purely spontaneous, and they subject the use of cunning to the scrutinizing eye of the intellect. Managers have to work out for themselves the actual cunning means by which to reach individual goals; constantly guided and inspired by their knowledge of the art of cunning, they can also draw on the valuable resources of their own intuition, intelligence, imagination, creativity, ingenuity, and, last but not least, factual knowledge, combined with characteristics such as presence of mind, cold-bloodedness, and often boldness.

Six categories of cunning techniques

As the 36 stratagems are derived from a broad concept of cunning, which also includes ruses that are free from deceit, they encompass a diverse range of behaviors. The first step is to carry out a rough stratagemic analysis, allocating each ruse to one of six basic categories of cunning. A refined stratagemic analysis can then be performed, attributing them to one of several of the 36 stratagems. Using this technique helps one to better understand ruses intellectually and, therefore, also on a practical level.

The Chinese "keyboard" of strategemical techniques with its 36 keys can be roughly divided into six basic categories.

1. ***Concealment stratagems***: Their purpose is to hide an existing reality, for example, stratagem 10, "Hiding the dagger behind a smile."
2. ***Simulation stratagems***: Their purpose is to lead someone to believe in something that does not exist, for example, stratagem 29, "Decorating a [barren] tree with [artificial] flowers."
3. ***Disclosure stratagems***: Their purpose is to uncover something that cannot easily be ascertained, for example, stratagem 13, "Beating the grass to startle the snakes."
4. ***Exploitation stratagems***: Their purpose is to make use of a situation that one has instigated oneself, or that just happens to have occurred, for example, stratagem 20, "Clouding the water to catch the fish [robbed of their clear sight]."
5. ***Stratagem-linking***: Two or more stratagems used cumulatively, or one after the other, lead to the goal.
6. ***Escape stratagems***: Their purpose is self-protection by avoiding a precarious situation, for example, stratagem 36, "[When the situation is growing hopeless,] running away [in good time] is the best stratagem."

In the case of the technically hybrid stratagems that do not only belong to one of the six categories, I do not give them their own individual category. It should be noted that only the stratagems belonging to categories 1 and 2 are based on deception. I call them "deception stratagems." However, the stratagems in categories 3 to 5 are not intrinsically based on deception. They are "presence stratagems," which rely on the skillful manipulation of ambiguous multileveled and multifaceted reality, full of opportunities. Anyone who equates cunning with lies/deception/cheating/untruth/ dishonesty encourages partial blindness to cunning, because they are unable to recognize the rich wealth of stratagems that are devoid of deception.

Four ethical categories of cunning

Cunning in itself is merely a tool. In the same way that a car can be used as a life-saving means to transport a critically ill patient to hospital, but also for a bank robbery, cunning can serve good, but also bad, purposes. The fact that here in the West we actually all accept trickery that is used for good purposes can be demonstrated by our reaction to Grimm's fairy tales. Hansel and Gretel use cunning to kill off the witch. Even the brave tailor kills the two giants using trickery. In cases like this, the use of cunning does not bother anybody. This shows that we also see cunning as a morally neutral instrument, just like a car. This remark has nothing to do with a theoretical justification of the sentence "The end justifies the means," but points only to the fact that in the Western world the use of cunning that serves a good purpose is *spontaneously* applauded. In fact, we take it for granted that trickery that serves the good is mostly approved. It is just when Westerners start theorizing that they often feel uneasy, because they perceive cunning *in itself* as a horrible, fiendish tool. However, this unrealistic theoretical Western condemnation of cunning by no means reflects life in the Western world itself, which is full of cunning. However, Western cunning is unfortunately mainly the result of a gut instinct, and thus without reflection and without theory, with no regard to wisdom and intelligence, and with no scientific foundation.

In considering the purpose of cunning from an ethical point of view, four different categories can be distinguished.

1. ***Damage stratagems***: The destructive egotistical element prevails.
   Example: the stratagems used by white-collar criminals.
2. ***Service stratagems***: These have a constructive purpose.
   Example: the quick-witted use of the *kairos* stratagem 12, "Leading the sheep away," for the purpose of recognizing and exploiting business opportunities.
3. ***Joke stratagems***: In this case, ruses are used to amuse.
   Example: joke articles stocked by a department store. Joke stratagems in business still appear to be barely recognized and developed, particularly in the area of advertising, which is generally much too serious.
4. ***Ethically hybrid stratagems***: This is an area where it really isn't clear whether the stratagem is destructive or constructive, whether one should laugh or cry.
   Example: certain Benetton advertising campaigns. These caused a sensation because of their cunning shock tactics (use of stratagem 13, "Beating the grass to startle the snakes"), and were successful in this respect, but they did make people feel uneasy.

When I speak of "damage," "service," "joke," and "hybrid" stratagems, I mean in each case the applications of stratagems and by no means the 36 stratagems themselves. The 36 stratagems remain ethically neutral and cannot be classified ethically. Judgment on ethical grounds can only apply to their application. Each of the 36 stratagems can be used constructively, destructively, to amuse, or in an ethically hybrid manner. As long as there is no internationally accepted "world ethos" that is recognized by all 6 billion people, the evaluation of the application of stratagems will be no more unanimous. Depending on the viewpoint that one adopts, opinions will differ. If I say "destructive" or "constructive," I mean this from the point of view of the general standards of decency and morals that currently prevail among the Western middle classes.

Destructive stratagems often lead only to tactical, hence short-term, results. In many cases, constructive stratagems have a strategic, that is, long-term, effect. A contemporary Chinese author explains this as follows:

> By their nature, stratagems are merely a means to an end, they are simply tools, which are themselves devoid of any ethical coloring … Anybody can use stratagems. But depending on the morality and honesty of the stratagem user, he [the user] may be noble or despicable. Stratagems hatched by malicious people may be crowned by success for a short time, but are ultimately doomed to failure. Only honorable people can secure long-term gains based on stratagems and be victorious in the end.[13]

The Chinese have been making observations like this for over 2,000 years. For instance, Liu Xiang (77–6 BC), voiced his opinions in particular with regard to politics:

> There are honest and dishonest stratagems. The stratagems of the nobleman are honest, the stratagems of the little man are dishonest. The stratagems of the honest man strive for the general good. If the honest man fights wholeheartedly for the people, he means it sincerely. The stratagems of the dishonest man derive from egotism and his pursuit of profit; if he does something for the people, it is lies and deception.[14]

Destructive applications of stratagems should of course be discouraged. They bring no lasting value in the end, particularly not for the stratagem user. This has been proven by numerous scandals that have blown up recently, in which managers acting in a malicious way were embroiled—think about the Enron scandal, for example. Better not to use a stratagem, and so pass up success in the short term, than to use a destructive stratagem from which one cannot really derive any pleasure, even if it is successful. Stratagems should only be used from ethically irreproachable motives.

The anthropologist Volker Sommer was certainly not far wrong when he made this observation, which can be extended to cover destructive stratagems: "We only hear about swindles that are busted. The majority remain undetected" (*Der Spiegel*, no. 18, 1992, p. 275). It cannot be denied that there are also stratagems that are effective in the very long term, successful and constructive from the point of view of the stratagem user, but destructive from another point of view. Just to name one example, "large-scale forgeries" undertaken by representatives of the Catholic Church in the first millennium AD endured over the centuries and cemented papal power to a certain extent even up to the present day (Küng, pp. 106ff.). Every user of a damage stratagem hopes to be one of those crafty individuals who escape unscathed. But the knowledge of stratagem will continue to spread. As a result, there will be an increasing number of people who will be in a position to see through cunning, and, if they deem it destructive, to thwart it. And, in this way, the situation in which, metaphorically speaking, 100,000 naive sheep can be manipulated by 10 wily foxes will hopefully be reversed.

Stratagem Training

In this chapter, the 36 stratagems are introduced within the schema of the six technical stratagem categories. First of all, the "range" of the stratagem in question is outlined under the heading "Stratagem radius." Then, under the heading "Stratagem prevention," measures are sketched out that provide protection against the stratagem concerned. Under the heading "Stratagem risk," mention is made of dangers associated with the use of the stratagem. One or more examples follow in conclusion.

Concealment stratagems

A reality that is actually present is hidden from view: stratagems 1, 3, 6, 8, 10, 24, 25.

Stratagem 1:

(First translation variant) Crossing the sea while deceiving the heaven/(Second translation variant) Deceiving the emperor [by inviting him to a house by the sea that is really a disguised ship] and [thus causing him to] cross the sea

The stratagem helps a person "to cross the sea," in other words, to overcome a difficulty. It is used against the "emperor," in other words, against people who are in high positions, or against authorities. Hence, this stratagem can be aimed at the manager, whose subordinates apply it against him, or at the supervisory board, when the manager applies it against such a body. Nowadays, however, it is no longer just people in high positions who can be targets of stratagem 1. It can be used against people of all kinds (Yu 1993, pp. 4–5). Since this stratagem is not just throwing sand in the eyes of the "emperor," but also of the all-seeing "heaven"—in ancient China, the highest deity—in a modern interpretation it relates also to issues that are being played out under the eyes of the general public, audience, or customers, while at the same time they remain hidden.

The stratagem is aimed at exploiting a blind spot in the field of vision of the stratagem's victim, by smuggling clandestine activities into routine procedures that are generally visible, but no longer monitored very carefully, and thus carrying them out unseen. Similarly, it is aimed at slipping through the loopholes in an attentiveness that has already naturally or artificially become deadened—to do something that is actually quite inadmissible in front of everyone's eyes and get away with it scot-free.

Cloak-of-invisibility stratagem; in-public stratagem.

Stratagem radius

A measure that is political is concealed, in that it is represented as "purely economically motivated." Economists sometimes conceal their own political expressions of opinion by representing these as objective assessments that have allegedly been derived from analyses of economic circumstances.

A job reference is produced that is bursting with friendliness, but in fact conceals the truth behind the words, and conveys hidden warnings in the form of descriptions that do not excite suspicion.

In business transactions, the customer can be given all the facts in the early stages, but certain issues are stressed, while others are allowed to slip into the background so that they escape the customer's attention. The latter approves the deal on the basis of the issues that have received particular emphasis, whereupon everything goes off smoothly. Thus, there is hardly a customer who reads the fine print in contracts very carefully, and, indeed, even if they were to check it, only rarely would they understand it in every respect. Under this stratagem also fall piggyback offers, such as wristwatches with a perpetual calendar, which are not in fact really needed but are paid for (*Facts*, Zurich, no. 14, 2004, p. 51), or television and radio equipment with every possible technical refinement, which the average customer pays for without really noticing that they are doing so, even though they only require just a few of the equipment's functions.

People are put to sleep by means of sonorous phrases such as "peace process," "human rights," and "justice," so that others can undertake the exact opposite of that which these phrases concern. This does not attract much attention among the people—they think that the persons repeating the phrases do as they say. A German building tycoon, who has since been sentenced, in China is said to have been able to borrow huge sums by pretending to renovate historic buildings in Germany or to build welfare accommodation. By virtue of the social dimension of the buildings planned, the moneylenders had neglected to check on their economic feasibility. "In fact, the larger a company is, the easier it is to cross the sea while deceiving the heaven" (*RR*, April 17, 1994, p. 7).

In *hierarchies of all kinds*, stratagem 1 is implemented in accordance with the maxim "Go along with something outwardly, but resist it in secret" (*Yang feng yin wei*) (Yu 1993, p. 6). "Oppose something outwardly, but support it in secret" is a further variant of this stratagem.

In negotiations, one person tells a story to the other, for example, concerning a slow mover, so that the partner is given to understand that the opportunity now being offered to them to complete the deal will not be repeated (Yu 1994, p. 42). These kinds of allegories give the person who hears them the initial impression that some amusement is now being offered to them, and they listen with interest. When the story-teller arrives at the end of the story, they suddenly notice that they have not just been presented with an entertaining story and so been granted a short break, but that they have been steered towards the recognition of certain issues (Mauch, pp. 69–70). Those who saw the *Star Trek* television series in the sixties believed that they were able to relax and abandon themselves to an engrossing science-fiction story. In fact, without it being generally realized, it was purposefully directed towards a particular worldview. For entertainment was not the actual purpose of this program. Rather "it was then, as today, about moral issues," as Robert Justman, producer of the first *Star Trek* episode, reveals. Thus, in the sixties, the series was already showing a mixed-race crew, women in positions of leadership, and also the first kiss between a white person and a black person. In fact, the intergalactic-television cultural revolution only lasted from 1966 to 1969, but "enthuses millions of people around the globe up to the present day with its multicultural crew" (*C*, August 2, 2002, p. 31).

The all-around care of passengers flying with Singapore Airlines can be viewed from the perspective of stratagem 1. They receive such attentive service from the flight personnel that they hardly notice that they are on a flight, and before they know where they are, they have already arrived at their destination, in other words, "they have crossed the sea" (Wee, p. 8).

Stratagem prevention

However much one would like to disguise the facts in a masterly fashion, there is always a risk that a detail remains unconcealed. And this one small feature that has remained unconcealed can be detected by the intended victim of the stratagem, if they are sufficiently vigilant. As soon as a whisper of something suspicious is detected, it should be investigated. Where there is the smallest cloud of smoke, look for the fire! Make the leap from the first vague indication to possible later developments! Don't view the world in too bland and superficial a manner! Don't wear your routine glasses!

Always try to keep a comprehensive and up-to-date picture of what your competitors are up to. Purely as a precaution, and without any pangs of conscience, take preventive measures against possible attacks in accordance with the maxim "Better safe than sorry!"

Stratagem risk

Those who want to conceal something from the "heaven" run the risk of ultimately fooling themselves.

Examples

Only three days for joint-venture negotiations

The Chinese company A, which was planning a joint venture together with the German company B, invited B to China for the final negotiations. Previously, A had already sent a draft contract in Chinese to B, and B had already sent a draft contract in English to A. The Chinese side had not taken up any particular position on these two draft contracts, and so the German side imagined that the two drafts were in agreement and that the contract could therefore be finalized without any difficulty. Only when the three members of the German delegation had arrived in China did they establish that there were serious differences in interpretation regarding the definitive formulation of the joint-venture contract. The Chinese side had not given the Germans to understand that there were any difficulties when they invited them to China for the finalization of the contract. Thus, A had given the impression that everything would go without a hitch. In this manner, A had enticed B "over the sea." In fact, the contract was finalized, but only as a result of a forceps delivery involving very hard negotiations with extremely tight time constraints, a scenario for which the German side was not well prepared.[15]

How to keep one's own interests out of sight

"Everyone who starts a war does so under the banner of a 'just cause.' No one will ever proclaim that they are leading a war for an 'unjust cause.'" The actual interests for which a war is engaged are not made public as a rule, although they are the pivot around which everything turns. They are concealed by the emphasis placed on the "just cause." "Thus the Bush administration in America at the start of the twenty-first century has led a war against Afghanistan, and this has been under the banner of the 'war against terror.' This has been the 'just cause,' and for that reason it quickly received the support of many countries." In fact, it was, and still is, fundamentally about the national interests of America. "Very many facts testify that all military undertakings of America are closely linked with the interests of large American companies. Under the excuse of the 'war against terror,' America has penetrated into Afghanistan, where it has worked for the establishment of a regime friendly to America. Its end objectives are access to energy resources and the protection of its geostrategic interests. As Master Sun said, 'In war one acts for the sake of an advantage.'[16] This short profound sentence helps us to look past the haloes with which warmongers surround themselves, and so to identify their true faces. America may be good at 'deceiving the heaven to cross the sea.' However, thanks to the saying of Master Sun, it is easy to see past this delusion" (Yu 2003, pp. 9–10).

Stratagem 3:
Killing with a borrowed knife

This stratagem includes:
1. cutting out the opponent by means of the hands of others.
   - *Straw-man stratagem; proxy stratagem.*

借
刀
殺
人

2. damaging someone in an indirect manner, without drawing attention to oneself.

    Alibi stratagem; mastermind-behind-the-scenes stratagem.

Here we are talking primarily about any application of a stratagem in which the real actor remains unrecognized. Under certain circumstances, this stratagem can also be used under the full public gaze. In a broad sense, the stratagem involves the achievement of an objective that is supported by the ingenious use of a third party or borrowed resources (Yu 1993, p. 26; Yao, p. 26). In these circumstances, it is no longer a concealment stratagem, but rather an exploitation stratagem. Seen in this way, the stratagem has a hybrid nature.

From the Chinese point of view, there is nothing wrong in using internal conflict—in the case of a single business opponent—or conflicts between a number of competing Western opponents, as the "knife" for "killing off" unfavorable conditions (Yu 2003, p. 19).

Stratagem radius

Enthusiastically applauded by all children, the courageous little tailor in *Grimm's Fairy Tales* kills the two giants lying under a tree. He does this by throwing stones from the tree alternately at the two giants while they are sleeping. Eventually, they start fighting and kill each other, because each believes that the other had hit him while he was sleeping.

In its "*war against terror*" and al-Qaida in Afghanistan, "America has hired Afghans to fight against Afghans, and so has been able to keep its own losses relatively small" (Yu 2003, p. 18).

In *negotiations*, Chinese managers can invite a number of competing firms at the same time, if possible also in the same building (Fang, pp. 263–4), and thereby can threaten to conclude the deal with the competitor with whom they are negotiating in a nearby room. Westerners who are blind to devices of this kind feel that this is "very uncivil" (*HBR*, October 2003, p. 89). However, this has nothing to do with any ignorance of the rules of politeness. On the contrary, the Chinese here are using the threatening references to the competitor as the "knife" that they, quite impassively and by no means secretly, are putting to the throat of their opposite number in the negotiations. The latter can mitigate this stratagem by asking precise questions regarding the name of the competitor, their product, their terms for delivery and guarantees, and so on. Larger business deals always have to be approved by some kind of higher authority. Chinese negotiation leaders can use this approval that still has to be sought as a "knife," in order to extract concessions from the opposing party. If the opposing party does not give way, the approval will not be forthcoming.

In the course of negotiations, Chinese write down every word of the remarks made by the opposing party, and any contradictions and inconsistencies that they discover they hurl at the latter, thereby moving the course of the negotiations in their direction (Fang, p. 264). Insofar as they are using deficiencies of the opposing party's argument as weapons against the latter, they are "killing with the knife of the other party."

Stratagem prevention

Any spontaneous, impulsive actions in the spirit of the Chinese saying "Hardly have the eyes seen some injustice on the street than the hand grasps the sword so as to provide help" should be avoided. Rather, you should take a somewhat closer look at the situation, since otherwise you can be exploited with ease. You should not allow yourself to be used all too easily to serve someone else's interests, especially if the other person is expecting this to result in damage to a third party. Say no to the role of cannon fodder! Don't do other people's dirty work for them!

Stratagem risk

The borrowed "knife" can be blunt. If one casts out the devil with the help of Beelzebub, the end result can be damage to oneself.

Examples

Using the law as the "knife" against the very same law

If it is possible to find a condition or a loophole in a law, through which one is able to cancel out the purpose aspired to by the law, this can be seen as an application of stratagem 3. Thus, the aim of an American law was to forbid the import of products for which less than 50% of their constituent parts were manufactured in America. A Japanese factory had developed a product comprising 20 constituent parts. Nineteen of the constituent parts had been manufactured in Japan. Only one part—albeit an expensive part—had been imported from America. Some 50% of the value of all 20 parts could be attributed to the American component. In this manner, the Japanese company succeeded in using as many Japanese parts and resources as possible, while nevertheless exporting an essentially Japanese product into America legally (Lin, p. 30). In the same way, citizens of the People's Republic of China not infrequently study a law less for the purpose of being able to adhere to it meticulously, than to see what options it opens up for application of the stratagem "Killing with a borrowed knife," with the intention of circumventing it legally.

Practical constraints and expert opinion as the knife

If someone justifies drastic measures in terms of what are alleged to be objectively inherent necessities, to rebel against which would indicate a loss of reality, or relies on the reports of recognized scientific experts, and in this way strangles protests and objections, this can be considered to be an application of the stratagem "Killing with a borrowed knife" (Li, p. 179). The application for membership of the World Trade Organization may well have served many politicians in the People's Republic of China as a knife for the "killing" of uncomfortable objections against drastic reform measures, and could still do so in the future.

Stratagem 6:
Clamor in the east, attack in the west

The attack is announced in the east, but is in fact pursued in the west; a skirmish is contrived at one location, but the real attack is at another location. Here east and west can represent any kind of differing or opposing directions or orientations. Attack can mean any kind of action. As a result of the clamor, the attention of the victim of the stratagem is diverted from the advance of the person using the stratagem.

1. (In the original sense)
    target- or objective-concealment stratagem;

2. (In a more general sense)
    diversion stratagem.

Stratagem radius

In *World War II*, the *Allies* fooled the Germans by pretending to attack using the shortest route across the English Channel, when in fact they landed much further away in Normandy. This application of stratagem 6 was of strategic significance.

In certain *computer games* or *sports*, the attention of the opponent is diverted to a particular point so as to launch a surprise attack at another location.

In *negotiations*, party A diverts attention to a subject that, in fact, is unimportant to them. If A later signals a willingness to be flexible on this subject, party B will be pleased with their apparent success in the negotiations. As a quid pro quo, B concedes on some matter that is genuinely important for A (Yu 1994, pp. 45–6).

As a *questioning technique*, someone can pose a long series of completely trivial questions ("clamor in the east"), in order to suddenly inquire without warning about something that is very sensitive ("attack in the west"). There is always the chance that the other party will answer the question in exactly the same spontaneous way as all the harmless questions they have answered previously.

With the cry of "Stop thief!"—think of false announcements of a terrorist attack, false tip-offs in relation to any kind of investigation, or pointing to the misdeeds of others—crooks of all kinds can very easily divert attention from their own activities.

Trick thief: "A brief diversion of attention, and the briefcase has already disappeared. This happened in Terminal B of Zurich-Kloten Airport. A 61-year-old British man was spoken to in the arrivals hall. As the unknown person took their leave, the crocodile-leather briefcase that was on the baggage cart was also missing. Contents: gold wristwatches, flight tickets, and cash. Value of the haul: some Sfr45,000" (*20 Minuten*, Zurich, August 14, 2001, p. 3).

Stratagem prevention

Where there is a scene of great commotion or unusual events, do not become transfixed like the rabbit by the snake. Instead, allow your gaze to sweep around the scene as a precaution. If someone falls to the floor in a station concourse, you naturally hurry to help them. But put your bag down in such a way that that you can keep it constantly in sight. For it could indeed be the case that an accomplice or an opportunistic thief is using the confusion to steal the bag. If the opponent is behaving in a completely different manner than one would oneself in the same situation, one must ask oneself whether they are perhaps up to no good, and take care accordingly. Before entering into negotiations, you should study the real needs of the opposing party as accurately as possible, so that the latter is not able to lead you to believe in any pseudo-needs. One should always keep the essentials in view, and not allow oneself to be diverted by secondary matters.

Stratagem risk

If you try out the deviation maneuver on an opponent who is wide awake, you play immediately into their hands.

Example

Piracy-fighting versus sabers

At the time of the Ming dynasty (1368–1644), Japan bought from China a certain number of sabers every year. So as not to allow the Japanese military capability to become too strong, the Chinese imperial court issued a declaration that no more than 3,000 sabers could be sold to Japan in each year. In the year 1507, the Japanese envoys presented a demand to the Chinese government that they should sell 8,000 sabers. This was refused by the Chinese. Now, an experienced Japanese diplomat, over 80 years old, came forward and said threateningly, "If you will not sell us the 8,000 sabers, we will cease to do business altogether. We will return immediately to Japan. Pirates, who at the present time we are holding in check, will once again infest your coasts."

The Chinese imperial court feared the Japanese pirates, against whom it was incapable of taking effective action because of its own military weakness. They constantly infested and plundered the Chinese coasts. China was dependent on the support of Japan for any effective fight against the pirates. The Chinese government therefore gave way and sold the Japanese the 8,000 sabers they had asked for.

A Chinese stratagem researcher explained the Japanese negotiating success in light of stratagem 6. In the face of the Chinese refusal, the Japanese no longer insisted on the 8,000 sabers. Instead, they brought up a totally different matter, namely, the threat from the Japanese pirates (Yu 1993, pp. 59–60). Thus, the Japanese made "clamor in the east," in order finally to "attack in the west," in other words, to complete the planned purchase successfully.

Stratagem 8:

Openly repairing the [burned wooden] walkway, in secret [before completing the repairs] marching to Chencang [to attack the enemy]

暗
度
陳
倉

1. The stratagem of the disguised march direction.
   Second-route stratagem; detour stratagem.

2. Concealing the real malevolent intention behind public activities that seem harmless and completely normal.
   Normality stratagem.

The direct path of attack is blocked. The enemy is keeping it under surveillance. There is, however, another route that is not being observed by the enemy, or is unknown to them. In the historic example from the year 206 BC, Chencang—which was not under enemy observation—lay about 320 kilometers from the end of the wooden-walkway route—which was kept under surveillance by the enemy.

The stratagem succeeds if the enemy thinks only within the framework of the known route. Therefore, they do not monitor another route that stands open to the enemy. In contrast to stratagem 6, in stratagem 8 it is not so much the target of the attack, but the route of the attack, that is selected in a disguised or ingenious manner. When translated to the business world, the stratagem often involves the visible utilization of a path from A to B with, at the same time, the secret utilization of a path from A to C, or simply the utilization of a path that is unremarked by the opposing party. Look into the nooks and crannies of a reality that is for the most part complex, positively seek out the solution paths that are hidden from the gaze of the slow movers, and adopt them with determination! Search out with a trench periscope the potential for rescue from a position that initially seems to be hopeless. Discover doors where others see walls!

Stratagem radius

The *Falungong* group—seen by the West as a harmless meditation movement, but from the official Chinese viewpoint as a dangerous sect, and therefore forbidden—has succeeded several times in infiltrating minute-long propaganda messages directly into the transmissions of official local Chinese television channels. That the Falungong seek publicity was well known. However, the authorities were obviously unaware of certain technical paths into the programs of the public television authorities. The Falungong therefore succeeded in reaching their objective by a route other than that controlled by the authorities, a publicity success that was also noted internationally.

In a cartoon, a functionary sits at a desk in an office. On the other side of the desk, another official is hard at work, writing a document. Before the functionary stands a man who obviously has a request to make. In order to get to the point more quickly, he has brought with him a large string bag full of goods. He clearly wants to present this to the functionary. However, the latter raises his left hand to ward him off, and says, "For us, the deplorable custom of offering presents is frowned on here!" At the same time, though, he reaches out towards the visitor under the desk, with a note in his other hand. On this can be read "My home address is ..." The cartoon has the caption "Marching secretly to Chencang."

Stratagem prevention

"What every man holds to be agreed, most deserves to be investigated" (Georg Christoph Lichtenberg). If you are convinced that you have the only route that stands open to the opponent completely under surveillance, you should nevertheless not be lulled into a false sense of security. Rather, you should put yourself in the position of the opponent, and look for the alternative routes that are at their disposal. If the area to be secured has an uncertain boundary, you should take precautions in as many directions as possible, so that no kind of loophole is exposed to the opponent. You should keep under full and continuous surveillance the opponent's movements in all directions.

Stratagem risk

Instead of leading to the desired objective, the second route could lead in the wrong direction.

Example

Joint-venture negotiations for information-gathering

Americans wanted to know whether a certain Chinese harbor was being used for military purposes. In order to find this out, they entered into joint-venture negotiations with Chinese partners regarding an extension to this harbor. The Americans used the negotiations to find out what the real functions of the harbor were. Finally, they established that it really was a harbor for merchant shipping. At that point, they broke off the joint-venture negotiations. The joint venture used as a stalking device by the Americans was "the repair of the wooden walkway," but by a secret route they arrived at "Chencang," in other words, at certain information.

It is said of the Japanese that they frequently prolong negotiations concerning a joint venture or other forms of investment. Here the real purpose is alleged to be often not about reaching a business agreement, but about using the negotiations for industrial espionage. The Japanese had been carrying out negotiations of this kind with a company in the province of Anhui, but only to find out the production secrets of the high-quality Xuan paper used for traditional Chinese painting and calligraphy. The result was that the Chinese lost their unique know-how, and that "today the best Xuan paper in the world is manufactured in Japan" (Li, p. 207).

Stratagem 10:
Hiding the dagger behind a smile

Evil intentions are hidden by outward friendliness, fine words, and courteousness.
Stratagem of two tongues; Janus-head stratagem.

The "smile" can consist of a pretended honesty and false sympathy, by means of which one activates true honesty and true sympathy in the opposing party, in order to profit thereby (Chen 2, p. 103).

Charm offensives and destruction can occur in succession. However, one can only deal in this way with an opponent with whom the differences are not too great, and who likes to be "stroked". Faced with a brutal opponent, whose head cannot be turned, this stratagem will quickly fizzle out.

With regard to business life, a distinction can be drawn between two constructive applications of this stratagem. The first is related to PR activities in particular, and is to be understood in the weakened sense of "Conceal true intentions behind a smile" (Yao, p. 78). The second is related, for example, to negotiations, and involves being friendly and soft in outward appearance, but uncompromising and hard in inner resolve. This corresponds to the Latin saying *Suaviter in modo, fortiter in re* ("Gently in manner, but unyielding in matter").

Stratagem radius

In about 1763, during the *French and Indian War*, on the instructions of the British commanding officer Jeffrey Amherst, blankets contaminated with smallpox were distributed to Indians (*Die Zeit*, January 24, 2002, p. 16).

In the first years of his presidency, François Mitterrand succeeded in almost suffocating a once mighty French Communist Party by means of an intensive hug (*WW*, January 11, 1996).

In email messages, computer viruses are distributed under names such as "I love you" (Li, p. 217).

Stratagem prevention

A long time ago, Confucius warned, "Soft words and ingratiating expressions are rarely paired together with humanity." One should react with caution to statements of friendliness from an unknown person, and even more so when they come from an opponent. You should be careful of attractive things whose origins are opaque. Beware of flatterers!

Stratagem risk

If the "smile" appears artificial, it can be counterproductive and awake mistrust. The "dagger" is then not fully hidden (Yu 1993, pp. 86–7). If you use stratagem 10 against a merciless opponent, you run the risk of finding yourself ranked even lower in this person's estimation, and of provoking them to even harsher measures.

Example

The enthusiastic reception

On account of an important piece of business, the general manager (A) of a French company flew personally to Japan, in order to be present at the negotiations at the highest level. The flight lasted 13 hours. Shortly before arrival in Japan, the exhausted A said to his companions that what he needed after landing was a refreshing shower and some reinvigorating sleep: "We won't go anywhere other than straight to the hotel." However, he had hardly left the gangway of the aircraft when he was met by a smartly dressed young man. With overflowing politeness, the latter said that the general manager (B) of the Japanese company had organized an evening banquet to welcome the foreign guests. He was waiting impatiently for the arrival of the delegation. With these words, the young Japanese man bowed again another time. His effusive friendliness ruled out any kind of negative reaction. Thus, there remained nothing else for A and his companions to do than to make their way to the banquet. Food and drink were provided in abundance, and the friendliness of the Japanese host exceeded all expectations. A was soon no longer able to count how many Japanese had already drunk his health, and how often his glass had been refilled with alcohol. Indeed, he had a very pleasant evening. Only late into the night did he arrive at his hotel. Very early on the next morning, there was a knock at his door. A messenger informed him that the Japanese negotiating delegation had already been waiting a long time for him. A washed quickly and hurried to the site where the negotiations were to take place. The Japanese were all fresh and fully rested, whereas he and his companions were still half-dazed from the previous night. Small wonder that he came off second best in the subsequent negotiations. In the extremely friendly reception of the Japanese, the hidden intention was to trip him up (Yu 1993, p. 91; Yao, pp. 79–80).

Stratagem 24:

假
道
伐
虢

Borrowing a route [through the country of Yu] for an attack against [its neighboring country of] Guo [, in order to capture Yu after the conquest of Guo]

Two-stage stratagem; double-objective stratagem, whereby both objectives can only be achieved with the aid of the opponent, but only the first harmless objective is exposed to them, whereas the second objective that is fatal for them is concealed; *stratagem of end-objective concealment.*

In the business sector, this stratagem can be understood in its original sense when, for example, company A enters into a tie-up with company B, and then, thanks to this increase in strength, clears company C out of the way, in order to cause B to disappear at a later date, too. In addition to this literal interpretation of the stratagem, it is sometimes simply the idea of "borrowing a route" that is emphasized. Thus, if one finds an unusual route for solving a problem, this can also be seen as an application of stratagem 24 (Lin, p. 136).

Stratagem radius

Hegel (1770–1831) formulated the expression "the cunning of reason" (*Strategeme 2*, pp. 335ff.). Example: A person is out to make mischief, but in the last resort—against the will of the person concerned—something good comes out of it. Did not Dietrich Bonhoeffer say, "I believe that God, out of everything, even the worst evil, can and wants to allow good to emerge"? One could refer back to the Cultural Revolution (1966–1976) that was orchestrated by Mao Zedong. The ideal of the rule of law was at that time trodden underfoot; law and order were to a large extent abolished. This objective was achieved by

Mao. However, in the longer term, the terrible results of the negation of the law caused by the Cultural Revolution made the Chinese in the higher echelons aware that they could not do without laws. Thus, Mao achieved something that he did not want to achieve, but—from Hegel's point of view—that the cunning of reason achieved via the circuitous route of Mao's activities in China.

It is expressly the effectiveness of the "cunning of reason" that Michael Stürmer counts on, when he hopes that via the introduction of the euro "the Europeans will be forced into a greater political capability and integration than the politicians were able to create between Maastricht 1992 and Amsterdam 1997" (*NZZ*, February 20, 1998, p. 5). For "behind the European monetary union stands a political cunning, to which the European Union owes many of its earlier successes and even its birth: The interests of commerce and industry in large-scale liberalization have been used as the engine for the political unification of Europe" (*Der Bund*, Bern, May 4, 1998, p. 5). Seen from the point of view of stratagem 24, that is to say: Economic forces have been used to eliminate independent national initiatives in the economic dimension in Europe. That made general sense, and all were more or less happy to go along with it. The end effect has been, however, that the nations of Europe have also been politically emasculated. Not everyone who was striving for economic unification really wanted this to happen, though. Political unification will, nevertheless, as a result of the forces resulting from economic unification, be inescapable and inevitable. "The unity of the economic entity, social entity, and the nation state" will be dissolved by the euro, and "the instruments of earlier national monetary policy—interest rates and exchange rates" will be taken away from the nation states (Werner Weidenfeld, *NZZ*, July 10, 1998, p. 5). Seen in hindsight, therefore, the measures carried out in full public view for economic unification (such as the introduction of the euro) served at the same time the concealed objective, aimed at by certain far-sighted politicians, of a final political unification of Europe.

Stratagem prevention

In the case of an objective that you are striving for, or one that has been set by others, you should always ask yourself whether you are aiding and abetting the fulfillment of a higher-level concealed objective that you do not endorse, without wishing to do so. Whoever thinks in this way will be particularly vigilant when faced with so-called strategic alliances or mergers, and also when faced with other business collaborations. One must be aware that one's own greed, ignorance, and blind confidence can be starting points that predestine one to be chosen as the victim of stratagem 24 (Yu 1993, pp. 240–1). If you wish, according to a moderate interpretation of stratagem 24, to prevent the competition from "borrowing a route" to gain the upper hand, you should survey this route in a timely manner and monopolize it yourself if necessary.

Stratagem risk

The "route" that one "borrows" oneself can mean that one is barking up the wrong tree.

Example

Mr. Li announced in an advertisement that he wished to sell an apartment. He had in mind a price of $50,000. Interested parties who replied to the advertisement offered $30,000, $35,000, and $40,000. Just as Mr. Li was starting to examine the offer of $40,000 more closely, a new customer replied with an offer of $45,000, and wanted to pay $5,000 on account immediately. Mr. Li was of course very happy with $45,000. For this reason, he accepted the bid of the latest party. At the same time, he sent a rejection to all the others. And now he waited for the completion of the deal. But nothing more was heard from the buyer who was in pole position. After several days, Mr. Li could not hold out any longer, and he reached for the telephone. The other shocked him with the information that his wife thought that $45,000 was too much. She had already found a cheaper apartment somewhere else. Could one perhaps negotiate over the price once again?

Mr. Li was naturally beside himself. However, he had to swallow his anger. For his opposing party was now the only person remaining who was interested. And Mr. Li wanted to be rid of his apartment as quickly as possible. Thus, there remained nothing else open to him than to start to renegotiate the price. Finally, an agreement was reached at $30,000.

By means of his high offer, which was not seriously meant, the buyer had first of all entrapped Mr. Li and induced him to turn away all the buyer's competitors. Now the buyer was suddenly in a strong position, while the seller's hands were tied. Thereupon the buyer defeated the seller and extracted a favorable selling price—from the Chinese point of view, a typical example of the application of stratagem 24 (Yu 1993, pp. 247–8).

Stratagem 25:

偷
梁
换
柱

Stealing the beams and replacing the pillars [on the inside, while leaving the facade of the house unchanged]

Taking the soul from a body, but leaving the body intact.
Hollowing-out stratagem.

With stratagem 25, the content of an object is secretly changed, usually for the worse. Seen from the outside, everything remains the same, but the appearance is deceptive. In the German language, the talk is sometimes of a "labeling swindle" or "deceptive packaging."

Possible subjects for hollowing out are any kind of object, company, or organization that remains the same externally, but has been remodeled internally—also quotations, whose wording has not been touched, but whose content has been modified.

Stratagem radius

By means of the acquisition of a majority stockholding without much fuss, the ownership relationships of a company are altered, while the company outwardly appears to remain the same. As an example, one might cite the Hong Kong tycoon Li Ka-Shing (born 1928) (Chen 2, pp. 259–60), who—from the Chinese point of view, quietly and secretly, and primarily through the purchase of stock—acquired Hong Kong companies previously owned by British stockholders—and so converted them into Chinese companies. In this manner, and also through other business successes, Li Ka-Shing has become—with an estimated fortune of $15 billion—one of the richest men in the world.

A hairdressing salon that continuously remodels its old services, and replaces or expands them with new services, such as photographing customers who have just had their hair done, is considered to be a user of stratagem 25. Seen from the outside, it is always the same business, but when the customers go inside, they are always coming across surprises (Yao, pp. 200ff.). The replacement of old material by new material in the manufacturing of a basic commodity that externally remains the same is seen as an implementation of stratagem 25 (Yu 1994, pp. 204–5).

If an old team of managers has to step down from a governing board, it can use stratagem 25 in such a way that, when it is faced with this hollowing-out of the board, it ensures that it is succeeded by people who think in exactly the same way (Yan, p. 75).

In negotiations, the application of stratagem 25 can consist of suddenly replacing a first delegation and confronting the opposing party with new people. In this way, concessions that have already been made can be recovered, points can be reset, delays can be brought about. Example: A Chinese manager first sends their subordinates into the negotiations with the brief to take a hard line. If the negotiations get bogged down, suddenly the boss surfaces in person and takes the negotiations in hand. Now, there is a good chance that the opposing party, who does not wish to forgo the business, views the appearance of a boss as a last lifeline, and correspondingly comes towards them in the negotiations, ready to make concessions.

Stratagem prevention

One should not let one's "beams" and "pillars" out of sight, one should know their status extremely well, and one should tend and care for them—also with an eye on one's allies. In discussions and negotiations, you should be on your guard for any hollowing out. If, for example, the opponent quotes a statement that you have made, you should listen to it very carefully. If they quote incorrectly or substitute a totally different statement, then you must correct this without delay. You should express yourself clearly and unambiguously, so that you do not aid or abet any hollowing-out of meaning in what you have said.

Stratagem risk

If one removes an opponent's "beams" and "pillars," this leads as a rule simply to the opponent's weakening, but not however to complete control over them or to their destruction. On occasion, you can even give the opponent the opportunity to get in new "beams" and "pillars," and finally to outdo the user of the stratagem. Something of this kind occurred with Germany, which after World War II lost very many "beams" and "pillars," but was thereby forced to build up new industrial facilities and so on, with the result that it rapidly regained a strong position.

Examples

Financial support from the sale of cars that were not owned

On April 14, 1988, a Chinese office of the Japanese electrical equipment company A and the Chinese machinery factory B concluded a leasing contract. According to this contract, company A leased to company B two Fengtian limousines for a period of 54 months for a sum of $31,000. Both vehicles were to be handed back to company A when the 54 months had expired. On April 30, 1988, company B received the vehicles, for which it was to settle the leasing costs in October 1989. Later, company B found itself in financial difficulties. In desperate straits, it sold both the cars for a high price. At the start of 1992, company B bought two vehicles of the same model that were almost ready for the scrap heap. On October 10, 1992, company A took back both cars. However, it discovered that the cars were extremely worn out. It called in a firm of attorneys. The latter brought the case before the court, and accused company B of having "stolen the beams and replaced the pillars," in that it had illegally disposed of the original cars and replaced them with vehicles that were ready for the scrap heap. The court awarded to the plaintiff and ordered company B to pay damages.[17]

In this case stratagem 25 was applied in a criminal manner and correspondingly sanctioned.

Antelope instead of venison

For 99% of unsuspecting customers, it is possible to replace dearer meat with a cheaper type of meat, and in this way to maximize profits. In numbers: Venison costs DM40 per kilo, antelope only DM10–20; between chicken and turkey there lay a 40% price difference, while separator meat was available at just 30 pfennigs per kilo (*FAZ*, November 16, 1998, p. B8). Thus, it came about that something was sold as venison that in reality was another, cheaper kind of meat. In order to protect themselves against stratagemic manipulation of provisions, Chinese customers sometimes make use of their own stratagemic countermeasures (see *Strategeme 2*, 25.9).

Simulation stratagems

You are led to believe a nonexistent truth: stratagems 7, 27, 29, 32, 34.

Stratagem 7:
Creating something out of nothing

The "nothing" is not a vacuum, but, for example, involves making a mountain out of a molehill (Chen 1, p. 74) or having a "crazy idea" that proves to be a gold mine (Chen 1, p. 78).
Creator stratagem.

Stratagem 7 is technically a hybrid, because it belongs to the simulation category of stratagem or the deception-free exploitation category of stratagem, according to circumstances.

a. For the most part, the stratagem is viewed as a simulation stratagem. You gain an advantage, while you create an illusion, a fake, or carry out a placebo transaction. The scope of this stratagem goes from legitimate exaggeration and praising a product to the point of lies and criminal deception (Yao, p. 55).

b. If stratagem 7 is used as an exploitation stratagem, then you can capitalize on an almost inexhaustible yet unexploited potential of the reality. By virtue of a constructive vision which you turn into reality, you achieve success or you can gain ground on an opponent. Particularly in economic life, this side of stratagem 7 is emphasized, because "the business war in reality is a creativity contest" (Chen 1, p. 79). You outdo the competition not by developing ideas within a routine framework but by dint of daring ideas penetrating into as yet unexplored areas of research and development, and with imaginative and creative forward-thinking. Aided by your imagination, you need to fathom and exploit the incredibly diverse character of what is real—something those dopey individuals who are blind to cunning fail to notice.

Intellectual openness to the whole world and interrelating thinking are in demand. "'History has no meaning,' said Karl Popper, only to add immediately, *so that we can give a meaning to it*" (*NZZ*, November 12, 2001, p. 27). As a human being, one is thrown into this world, without having been asked. It is the responsibility of each individual not to allow themselves to be held back too much by handicaps, but to take advantage of the possibilities, in order "to continually reinvent themselves." Through technical civilization, life may have been deprived of its mystique. We'll put the sparkle back into it—by means of noble goals that we set ourselves; by means of ideals that we build on; and why not by means of a religion, or through expressing delight over endearing trifles? "Reality is the illusion we make of it" (Günter Rohrbach, *FAZ*, November 29, 2001, p. 45).

Stratagem radius

Stratagem 7 as a simulation stratagem

In accordance with the motto *Xu xu shi shi* ("Empty, empty, full, full"), one mixes statements of truth with falsehoods, or one offers both genuine and imitation goods, and thus bewilders the opponent in such a way that false statements are also looked on as true ones, and imitation goods are taken to be the genuine article (Zhang, p. 76).

A shepherd boy, who watched over a sheep grazing on a hill, called for help, because a wolf had allegedly come. The people hurried up the hill, only to establish that the boy had made a fool of them. Later, the boy reenacted this scene repeatedly, but nobody took any notice of his cries for help. Then, when a wolf really appeared and the boy cried out in earnest, nobody came and the wolf ate the sheep. The person who craftily turns this story around, will repeatedly trigger a new false alarm—hence a "nothing"—in order to be able to carry out the deed later—hence a "something"— unhindered (Yu 2003, pp. 35–6).

A Taiwanese washing machine came only fourth in a consumer survey after three foreign makes. The problem with the washing machine was its poorly defined corporate image. The advertising agency handling the washing-machine factory's account discovered four small flaps in the washing drum, which were highly visible from the outside. The designers said that these small flaps were only fitted for aesthetic purposes and had no technical function. Of course, if one really wanted to ascribe them a function, the small flaps could be said to have a minute impact on the washing cycle. The advertising men and women then exploited this unusual feature of the washing machine. They created a brand-new name for this part of the appliance equipped with four small flaps, namely, "combined rotation mechanism," impressively described the positive effects of the "combined rotation mechanism" on the washing cycle, and thereby helped the washing machine to enjoy a sales boom (Chen 1, pp. 79ff.).

Pseudocustomers (*tuo*) are employed by Chinese businesses or stores. If a genuine customer stands indecisively in front of a product, they push to the front of the line and "buy" this same product, perhaps praising it to the skies, too, which the hesitant customer of course hears. The enthusiastic pseudocustomer is supposed to encourage the customer to make the purchase. This kind of pseudocustomer is found in China in different industries and variations (Yu 1994, pp. 234–5).

Creative accounting, bogus companies, phoney invoices, fictitious businesses; stock-market gurus, who (apart from their possible insider knowledge) don't really have any knowledge about the future, but make out that they know something; relying on their prestige, they liven up the atmosphere and so earn money—these are all forms of expression for stratagem 7.

A host of legends has grown up around the Rothschilds. The most famous is connected with the Battle of Waterloo on June 18, 1815. The London stock exchange eagerly awaited the outcome of the battle. Should Napoleon be victorious, then the values of long-term government bonds would fall. On the other hand, should the Corsican be defeated, then it was calculated that the consequence would be a rise in value. By means of their own ingenious messenger system, the Rothschilds succeeded in being the first to bring the news about Napoleon's defeat to Britain, which facilitated a stock-exchange coup, the like of which had never been known before. Rumor has it that Nathan Rothschild, the head of the London banking house, was present at the stock exchange building at that time, standing motionless in front of its "column." Secure in the knowledge of the outcome of the Battle of Waterloo, he didn't invest, but sold. The fate of the bonds appeared to be sealed. The more he sold, the heavier the fall in value. There was whispering in the corridors, "Rothschild must know: The Battle of Waterloo is lost." Until Nathan suddenly started buying, that is to say, at a price that he himself had determined. When the news of the victory reached London shortly afterwards, the price of papers rocketed. "The Rothschilds made millions."[18]

"*Rumors* are the most dreadful of phenomena. You can't see them; you can't apprehend them; they have no shadow and are shapeless— just wagging tongues determine your fate for better or for worse. A single sentence can drive a person to suicide and persuade a hero to surrender. With merely a rumor offensive, many an opponent was already eliminated, without the need to cross swords with them" (Chen 1, p. 73).

"If someone spreads an infamous statement about me and this statement is printed off by a reputable publishing house, then the statement becomes part of the reality according to the media, and each publisher copies it from the next" (Ringier publicist in chief Frank A. Meyer, *Das Magazin*, weekend supplement of the *TA*, no. 29, July 20, 2002, p. 12).

Exploitation stratagem

"Products are not manufactured to meet the needs of the consumer, but to create new needs for the customer," said Honda Soichiro (1906–1991), who was one of the most important industrialists in Japan, and whose enterprise, worth megabucks, produced the world's best-selling motorcycles (Yu 1994, p. 59).

A new application is invented for a product, for instance, by palming off combs on bald-headed monks to massage their itching scalps (Zhou 1992, p. 18).

The American light-entertainment industry holds global fascination by repeatedly inventing new fads and all kinds of fashion trends to banish boredom, which pleasure-craving people throughout the world can't abide, and to satisfy the need for entertainment.

Sharp-tongued individuals claim that the bakers' guild invented the feast of Epiphany, in order to counter the January drop in sales with unspectacular cakes (*Zürichsee-Zeitungen*, Stäfa, January 5, 2002, p. 25).

Stratagem prevention

If stratagem 7 crops up as a simulation stratagem, you're forearmed if you're not gullible. If you're too trusting, you're an easy target to be taken for a ride (Yu 1993, p. 64). Questioning can rarely do any harm. Skepticism is often healthy. The question of the "demystification" of the world indicates a so-called characteristic feature of modern society. But, in reality, it's just full of false charm. You shouldn't succumb to it. The insight gained from knowledge of stratagem 7 is a help, in that there's an infinite number of possibilities to set up scandalous constructs in the world, which dispense with every reality. Many "realities" are pure fantasy and, as such, can be unmasked and rendered harmless.

If a rumor circulates over a long period, there's little chance it can be dispelled. It follows that immediate action should be taken against a false rumor. Provided that there is the remotest chance you can get a word in (unfortunately, this is often not always the case with a powerful stratagem user), you should identify the stratagem by its name and, using stratagem 30, challenge the stratagem user to prove the accuracy of the rumor. On no account should the person affected by the false rumor express their opinion about its content, because by doing so they only help the stratagem user to spread the rumor further. With each superfluous word the person affected by the false rumor encourages an even wider circulation. An uninvolved third party should check a rumor, provided it seems important. If it is unverifiable, then no more notice should be taken of it; otherwise you will also become a stratagem victim. Crystal-clear information is the best way of preventing rumors. You should definitely proceed using the laws against criminal applications of stratagem no 7, such as slander, fraud, or counterfeit goods.

Stratagem risk

Making up rumors always leaves the perpetrator on shaky ground and can lead to boomerang effects. Behaving honestly is always the better way to achieve success, rather than blackening the name of the rival. In the analysis of enemies within the bounds of military, political, and diplomatic debates, using this stratagem is indeed sometimes seen in Chinese specialist literature as essential, but at the same time is described as a "double-edged sword," with which you can deal the enemy a heavy blow by skillful use of the stratagem, but with which you can also cut your own throat if you don't use it cleverly (Chen 1, p. 75). When you use stratagem 7 as an exploitation stratagem, you must be careful that a "great" idea doesn't prove to be a crazy one.

Examples

A legendary figure attracts money

The Japanese small town of Ina wanted to boost the "smokeless industry," namely, tourism. But to achieve this aim, some kind of tourist attraction was needed. To find such an attraction, the authority responsible set up a team, which streamed out in all directions around the town, gathering information about traditional customs and legends. In the course of its investigations, it chanced on the legendary local hero Kantaro, who was then thoroughly exploited. A little later, a giant statue of this local hero overlooked the town's railroad station. Suddenly, the bookstores were brimful of books about Kantaro's wonderful deeds, carried out for the benefit of the poor and needy. All kinds of devotional objects, such as reproductions of the hero's weapons and belt, as well as pictures and figures of him, were offered for sale, sprouting up like mushrooms. The town's inhabitants could even listen to songs about Kantaro. Indeed, the song "Kantaro of Ina" became a national hit. After a short time, the aim was achieved and the town became a major tourist destination (Chen 1, p. 75).

Increased growth thanks to insoles

Chinese businesspeople extol the virtues of needless shoe insoles with the dubious promise that they help the body to grow. Because of this, many Chinese men and women of small stature are induced to buy these insoles, and businesspeople grow rich. This kind of use of stratagem 7 is not approved of in China (*Satire and Humor*, Beijing, September 20, 2000, p. 5).

Stratagem 27:
Feigning madness without losing the balance

Here "madness" can mean a feigned mental or physical defect, or any weakness one is led to believe someone has. One affects not to hear, feigns illness, pretends to have frailties, in short, claims to have any deficiency.

1. Stratagem of a feigned mental or physical defect.
    Fools' stratagem; greenhorn stratagem; Till Eulenspiegel* stratagem.

2. Feigning ignorance, cluelessness, insignificance.
    Little-innocent stratagem; wallflower stratagem.

Even "naiveté" is a good thing. So, in certain situations you act like the good soldier Schweik. Or you pretend to be dead like a girl from Jena, who survived a rape in this way. By means of apparent simplemindedness, you stop your opponent functioning, in order to gain the upper hand at a critical moment or to get through a precarious situation. Or you act as if you don't understand what's going on; for example, when a transaction is anticipated or required, which you want to prevent or fend off. Under the guise of ignorance, you sabotage events. Sometimes it's clever to be silent, rather than talk stupidly. An understatement takes precedence over an overstatement. "Don't say everything you know, but always know what you say"—according to a well-known saying. "Sell more than you buy" (an Arab proverb), meaning say less and listen more to what the other person is saying. When negotiating, first let the other person talk and hide your own intentions (Yu 1994, p. 91). If necessary, assume a deadpan expression. By virtue of creative ignorance, in many cases you become a good conversation partner. If you didn't feign ignorance now and again, you would soon unnerve your conversation partners, telling you things you already

---

**Translators' note*: a reference to a medieval German peasant trickster, who often behaves like a fool.

know. Hiding one's light under a bushel is sometimes to be recommended, above all in the face of distrustful superiors, who are afraid that stratagem 30 could be used against them!

Stratagem 27 can be applied to superiors, beggars, troublemakers, and business competitors, but also to children and friends. From time to time, you forgive mistakes your children make, acting as if you haven't noticed anything. If you turn a blind eye and just let five mistakes go, you can perhaps let many an interpersonal thundercloud pass by, undisturbed. Sometimes it's advisable to grin and bear it.

Stratagem radius

When the American secretary of state *Henry Kissinger* pretended to have stomach pains during a visit to Pakistan in 1971, he was able to disappear from the scene very discreetly, and, unnoticed, undertook a flying visit to Beijing, where he prepared President Nixon's historic visit to China (1972).

Completely healthy employees sometimes take sick leave; some people pretending to be disabled collect disability benefits (*Strategeme 2*, pp. 454ff.).

Mao Zedong's successor *Deng Xiaoping* (1904–1997) formulated China's foreign-policy guidelines "for the next 50 years. They read 'Taoguang yanghui,' which means: For the time being, keeping a low profile and quietly developing one's own strong points" (*FAZ*, October 29, 2001, p. 48).

"Ignore it and sit it out" (*Badische Zeitung*, May 29, 2002, p. 1)— that was the maxim used by *Josef Blatter*, the head of FIFA (Fédération internationale de football association), in the face of severe accusations. In this way, he secured his dazzling reelection as FIFA boss.

When negotiating, sometimes the following is necessary: it's clever to be a bit stupid, for example, by repeatedly asking the same question, and perhaps addressing it to various members of the negotiating delegation on the other side. In this way, you may be able to spot weaknesses in their position.

Stratagem prevention

Acute observation of a seemingly weak opponent is important. If someone is constantly on sick leave, you can pay them an unexpected visit at home. Credulity is good, but checking is often better. Be on your guard against people who behave innocently!

Stratagem risk

Innocence can have a dubious effect and alert the opponent. If you feign naiveté and ignorance, confronted with your own inappropriate behavior, things might go wrong. Not everything can be resolved by turning a blind eye. Certain suppressed and unsolved problems are eventually too much for us, such as "illegal immigration, which we have closed our eyes to for a long time and have accepted" (*Die Zeit*, July 11, 2002, p. 3). Some things are not eradicated by hushing them up. Putting your hands over your eyes, ears, and mouth like the three monkeys, and seeing, hearing, and saying nothing, is sometimes dangerous in the long term. In European politics, the Kosovo conflict demonstrated where ignoring a crisis can lead (*Die Zeit*, November 18, 1999, p. 15), namely, to the outbreak of war in spring 1999. For a long time, Western states ignored atrocities committed by Saddam Hussein (*NZZ*, January 28, 2004, p. 2), with disastrous consequences. Silencing the prophet Cassandra can be lethal. If managers, hoping for better times, suppress the facts for too long in the face of a looming crisis, and do not implement countermeasures, that crisis can in general only lead to fatal results. The perception that the best way to deal with shortcomings is by concealment is sometimes wrong. On the contrary, examination of shortcomings can strengthen trust in the self-healing power of the system in question.

Example

The Japanese: Slow on the uptake

Three representatives of a Japanese aircraft company traveled to America, to negotiate a business deal. The American negotiating delegation consisted of numerous brilliant, highly qualified, high-ranking specialists. The Americans used the first round of talks, which began at eight o'clock in the morning, for a two-and-a-half-hour Hollywood-style presentation of their company, and of the products they wanted to sell to the Japanese. They used every technical aid at their disposal during their perfectly stage-managed company promotion. During the whole presentation, the Japanese said nothing. They sat still. After two and a half hours, the American delegation leader stood up, turned the light back on in the room, a broad smile on his face on account of the successful presentation. Then he turned towards the Japanese, and asked them, "Please tell me, what do you think?" A Japanese man, who smiled in an exceedingly friendly way, replied, "I haven't understood it yet." When the American heard that, he turned pale. "What do you mean by that? What didn't you understand?" Then another Japanese man started speaking, and said with extreme courtesy, "By and large, we didn't understand anything." The American almost lost his composure, but suppressed his anger and said, "From what point didn't you understand our presentation?" Then the third Japanese man spoke: "We understood nothing more from the moment the light went out and the slide presentations began." The American had to lean against the wall. He loosened his tie. He looked really despairing. Once again, he turned to the Japanese man: "Now then, um, er, so what would you like us to do now?" The three Japanese men answered, "Could you repeat the whole report?"

A Chinese commentator concludes: At the very moment when the Americans were convinced that their presentation had made a splendid impression, and believed that they could negotiate a high price with the Japanese, they had a tub of cold water poured over their heads. While the Japanese pretended to be stupid and asked for the whole presentation to be repeated, they destroyed the Americans' certainty of victory and their self-confidence. The Japanese controlled the situation. As a result, they succeeded in considerably depressing the price and concluding a good deal for themselves (Yu 1994, pp. 219–20).

Stratagem 29:
Decorating a [barren] tree with [artificial] flowers

The "barren tree" symbolizes a miserable reality; the "artificial flowers" stand for splendid resources that one can use to embellish the wretched facts. The main concern of the stratagem is not dissimulation, that is, the mere concealment of a nasty situation—although this aspect also plays a part—but pretending to have strengths, power, or significance, to be a threat, and so on; factors that, in truth and reality, are completely nonexistent.

Fake-blossom stratagem; impress stratagem; make-up stratagem.

Stratagem radius

In certain Chinese *department stores*, splendid escalators are installed. Yet, for over 300 days in the year they are motionless, displaying the notice "Under repair." They only start operating again on public holidays. In reality, the escalators are not so much serving the customers as fulfilling the function of mere decoration and image-building ("Escalators pretend to be ill," *RR*, August 30, 1995, p. 10).

The Chinese are very good at mounting a big show for foreign guests, with a throng of flag-waving; children singing songs along the road; the presentation of model enterprises; wonderful banquets;

streets made clean and spruced up, specially for the visiting day; and so on. In this way, creating a euphoric atmosphere can be effective, especially with Western businesspeople, and conducive to making commitments (Brahm, pp. 83–4).

In a Shanghai department store in 1982, a new range of sets of six high-stemmed, beautifully shaped wineglasses of the best quality was introduced. They were scarcely noticed on the shelves. Only between two and three sets a day could be sold. Later, some young salespeople came up with an idea. They filled the wineglasses with water, into which they poured a few drops of red ink. Now the previously transparent, colorless glasses suddenly acquired an aura; they appeared to be filled with wine and attracted the attention of the customers. Daily sales rose to 30–40 sets.

Other publicity measures that give a product a wonderful aura are regarded as applications of stratagem 29 (Zhou 1992, p. 92; Ye, pp. 286–7; Chen 1, p. 294), for example, the enhancement of a product's appearance with a display-window decoration or packaging (the Japanese are true masters at this); clever lighting; exploitation of large events or other functions; endorsement by genuine or so-called experts; and the association of a product with a famous personality. Department stores adorn themselves with cheap special offers on good quality products to entice customers—with the ulterior motive that they will still spend their money in other departments, too (Yu 1994, p. 54).

There's a suspicion that in America "several *electricity and gas suppliers* have inflated their turnovers through 'creative accounting'" (*Handelsblatt*, May 23, 2002, p. 14). The telecommunications giant *WorldCom* "inflated the profit," while it "entered current costs as investment" (*TA*, June 23, 2002, p. 23). In this way, the profits were "inflated to almost $4 billion" (*Zürichsee-Zeitungen*, July 23, 2002, p. 17). "Between 1999 and 2001, massive turnovers were embellished and costs hidden, resulting in artificial profits of more than $11 billion" (*NZZ*, March 3, 2004, p. 21). Using the stratagem was in vain. For a little later, WorldCom shocked investors and employees worldwide with the heaviest bankruptcy in American history. Assets worth $180 billion were wiped out.

In Britain, *herd numbers* were temporarily inflated—in order to gain subsidies (*NZZ*, March 28, 2001, p. 60).

Humanitarian aid: About 150,000 refugees seemed to have disappeared in Guinea. In the Kolomba camp, where previously 25,000 refugees had been looked after, according to official figures, the UN High Commission for Refugees found only 3,000 people. The following is the most likely explanation for this massive discrepancy between statistics and reality: "The figures for displaced persons had been deliberately inflated. There are various reasons for this. One reason could be that surplus aid was exchanged for cash on the market, which could then be used for personal gain or even to provide weapons for a guerrilla army. Another reason could be that, in such areas, a large proportion of displaced people are registered as refugees. This status not only gives them access to aid, but also efficient and free health care. And finally, inflating the figures also serves the interests of the aid organizations, which use such embroidered reports on their progress as the main instrument in their search for new funds" (*NZZ*, June 8, 2001, p. 7).

Investment cheats project a veneer of respectability, and thus take their victims for a ride. "So they invest a tidy sum in a distinguished address, glittering prospects, or impressive web pages. A frequently used device is membership of serious-sounding associations. In Germany, a company having their headquarters in Switzerland has the effect of inspiring confidence" (*SZ*, November 25, 2001, p. 85). Cheats inspect top restaurants and five-star hotels, right down to the last detail. Then they welcome their victims there and, by means of their familiarity with the locality—they know where the restrooms are, and supposedly even know the names of the chefs—convince them of their inherent respectability. So they adorn themselves with the ambience of luxurious surroundings, and thus project a veneer

of wealth and credibility, inducing their victims to put caution aside
(Zhou 1992, p. 91).

You can lend more weight to your own opinions in conversations
and publications, if you embellish them with quotations of great
intellectual standing. Don't forget: Fine feathers make fine birds!

Stratagem prevention

You must distinguish between the dazzling facade and the face that
could be hidden behind it. You must not be content with mere
facade—an all-too-respectable outward appearance should give rise
to mistrust. You shouldn't allow yourself to be overawed by splendid
statistics and impressive expert reports—they're often not worth the
paper they're written on.

Stratagem risk

If you lay it on too thick, it doesn't have the desired effect. If it's
temporarily dressed up, because you want to hide a short-term
inconvenience, the stratagem can succeed and remain undiscovered.
But if you try permanently to hide fundamental shortcomings with
an agreeable fake image, the ruse could turn out to be foolishness. So
it really is better to face the truth without cunning, tell everyone the
naked truth, roll up your sleeves, and bravely reform the system.

Examples

Mount Fuji with a curry summit, and the bank building with a giant Swatch

"Mount Fuji will change its appearance!" A few years ago, this was
proclaimed by the Japanese company SB. It announced that it was
going to use helicopters to scatter some of the yellow curry powder it
produced onto Mount Fuji's snow-white peak. The population
would then see Mount Fuji with a golden summit. With this

announcement, the company wanted to boost flagging sales of its curry powder.

But a storm of indignation immediately broke loose. The company SB was overwhelmed with criticism. The mass media condemned it in unison. After all, Mount Fuji was the symbol of Japan. How could the company SB allow Mount Fuji's head to be changed by substituting its own face!

This sharply worded reaction suited the company SB's plans exactly. It was the focus of general interest. By creating a lot of fuss about nothing, it had attracted general attention. After a while, the company SB hinted that due to intense disapproval in the Japanese press, it had reconsidered, and had reached the decision to abandon the plan to scatter curry powder onto Mount Fuji. At the same time, it expressed its feelings of regret to the Japanese people.

Then the people suddenly exclaimed, "Where there's great wealth, behavior is generous," "Tremendously powerful," and "Once it had recognized its mistake, it rectified it immediately," and the Japanese praised the company SB to the skies. The company's name was on everyone's lips. And in the end its curry powder flew off the shelves.

The company SB used Mount Fuji as the "tree"; it understood the importance of setting the scene for its "flowers," the curry powder, even though only in virtual reality and in an imaginary context, but evidently it was a very cost-effective exercise.

Similarly structured was a PR promotion for Swatch. The new Swiss watch was developed to ward off the Japanese wristwatch offensive, and it needed to become a household name. Nicolas G. Hayek, who was then adviser to the Swiss watch industry and later head of the Swatch group, describes how this happened: "Swatch's slogan was 'Highest quality, lowest price, for a challenging and fun-filled life,' and how did we get it across? Not by making ads costing us millions of Swiss francs—which, anyway, we didn't have—no! We 'got hold of' the most expensive skyscraper in Frankfurt's banking area—which, at that time, was the Commerzbank. Then, we convinced the president to hang a vast 140-meter working Swatch from the edifice of his bank. Initially, he thought we were all crazy—and pointed out that if the watch fell down onto the street, we would have a pile of dead bodies and injured people on our hands. Thereupon we also consulted the city fathers and city planners of Frankfurt (they were very cooperative), obtained their approval, and were eventually able to hang our colorful watch from the bank. Moreover, we wrote 'DM60, Swiss.' Nothing more. We let it hang there for four days—afterwards, every German knew what a Swatch was. And the entire caper cost us only about DM140,000. In this way, we promoted the message, the so-called Swatch message."[19]

Apple juice with sparkling mineral water, dressed up

Customers know nothing at all about the ingredients of many dishes. They buy the dishes, *because they are presented in a pleasing way*. Thus, sodium nitrite and ascorbic acid are used to dye sausage red. Apple juice with sparkling mineral water consists of 60% apple juice. It is mostly mixed from concentrates. Because the apple freshness is often lost in the process, it is dressed up with flavorings.

"Green parrot with red beak" instead of "spinach"

The Chinese emperor once paid a farmer an unexpected visit. The farmer could only offer him spinach to eat. So that the meal didn't seem so ordinary, it was given the name "green parrot with red beak" (*Hong zui lü yingwu*). The "green parrot" referred to the green spinach leaves, and the "red beak" to the reddish spinach stalks.

In the former East Germany, grilled or broiled chicken was known to be called *Goldbroiler* (from the English word "broiler"). In this way, a taste of the wider world was feigned.

Stratagem 32:

The stratagem of opening the gates [of a city that is unprepared for self-defense]

Stratagem of feigned ambush / risk; warning stratagem.

Stratagem of feigned harmlessness; all-clear stratagem.

This stratagem is the best known of all the 36 stratagems in China. It is in fact connected with a legendary use of the stratagem by an extremely popular commander and statesman of the third century BC (*Strategeme 2*, 32.1, 32.19). During a campaign, in the face of the unexpected, advancing enemy, this commander had the gates of the undefended city—in which he found himself without enough troops—opened, and furthermore calmly played his zither on the city wall within the opponent's field of vision. The opponent suspected an ambush and withdrew.

When using this stratagem in business life, it is handled according to need, so as to make the opponent believe that there's a "fullness" or an "emptiness," and to mislead them in this way to take certain actions.

Stratagem radius

In the *history of war*, sudden withdrawals of troops, combined with leaving behind empty tracts of land, have repeatedly aroused the opponent's suspicion, who thereupon withdraws, as the stratagem user wanted.

Within the framework of the *fight against crime*, bright lights or the sound of a radio are used during the night, in order to protect deserted houses from thieves.

As the Chinese see it, *authorities and departments* "sing the stratagem of the empty city," and outwardly give the impression that they're busy, but in reality are "empty," because the officials spend ages drinking tea somewhere, or otherwise whiling away their time.

When the People's Republic of China triumphantly entered the UN in the seventies, as a whole it played on the keys of stratagem 32 in a masterly fashion, according to a well-known Belgian sinologist (Simon Leys): to the whole world, it successfully gave the appearance of a future power; however, on looking more carefully behind the scenes, only poverty, backwardness, and an unstable regime were to be discovered (*Strategeme 2*, p. 623).

During a negotiation, the party which, behind the scenes, is in a desperate situation, and for whom the success of the transaction in progress is especially vital, can nonetheless behave in an indifferent and disinterested fashion towards the other party. They can, for example, get an employee to burst into the room in the midst of the negotiation to convey a false message that a business-class plane ticket for tomorrow's flight to Korea, where a business deal is to be negotiated, has just this moment been reserved. This gives the impression of their ability to conclude brilliant deals with other partners—all this to show no sign of weakness to the negotiating partner sitting opposite and, on the contrary, to gain from them the best possible contractual conditions (Zhang, pp. 325–6).

Stratagem prevention

If the opponent conspicuously and pointedly shows you an "emptiness" or a "fullness," you should analyze these comprehensively. If the "emptiness" or "fullness" presented cannot be verified, in spite of all attempts at clarification, maintain your position and patiently observe the opponent. Sooner or later, their stratagem 32 will fall victim to exposure.

Stratagem risk

A suspicious adversary will try to find out—and with reasonable certainty can quickly ascertain—whether the "emptiness" of the city is merely feigned or actually exists. Thus, the stratagem depends on the opponent's gullibility or how well-informed he is. It's a dangerous game and may easily go wrong. It is advisable to take supplementary measures to protect against the possible failure of this stratagem.

Example

Setting up a supply through the use of words

A small Chinese business needed raw materials for its production, and therefore entered into negotiations with a Hong Kong trader. The trader knew that the Chinese side had to rely on his raw materials as a matter of urgency, and wanted brazenly to reap the benefits of this fact. He demanded an outrageous price and, in addition, behaved arrogantly. Luckily for the Chinese side, the trader didn't know that their supplies would last for only another two weeks. Without a supply of the raw materials, the Chinese business was facing a halt in production. Although the representative of the Chinese side used all his customary negotiating skills, the Hong Kong trader didn't budge an inch from his hard line and was even aggressive. In the middle of this hopeless situation, the Chinese man suddenly thumped on the table and got up abruptly. Seething with rage, he said, "If this deal really doesn't matter to you, then you can leave now. We have enough stock for a whole year's production. Furthermore, we plan to switch over to a different product in a year's time. Then we'll no longer have to rely on you anyway. Sir, it was my pleasure!" And, with these words, he showed the Hong Kong trader the door. The trader was totally flabbergasted. His hopes seemed to have been dashed. The threat of the total loss of any profit loomed. After he had calmed down, he sat down again and now began to negotiate with the Chinese man in earnest. A mutually satisfactory transaction was agreed on by both sides.

A Chinese commentator concludes: The Chinese side found itself in an extremely vulnerable position here, the catastrophic extent of which was admittedly unknown to the Hong Kong trader. The Chinese man deceived him by virtue of the harsh words he used. He pretended to the Hong Kong trader that fullness dominated, where, in reality, almost total emptiness prevailed. In this way, he gave a real shock to his opponent, who of course didn't want to leave empty-handed, and this caused him to get off his high horse. If the Chinese man had really come clean about the desperate state of his business, then the Hong Kong trader would only have exploited this all the more mercilessly (Yu 1994, pp. 272–3).

Stratagem 34:
The stratagem of the suffering flesh

苦肉計

The self-mutilation stratagem (inflict injury on oneself to win the enemy's trust).

1. *Sham-deserter stratagem*;

2. *victim-status stratagem*; *sympathy-vote stratagem*;

3. *self-castigation stratagem*; *appeasement stratagem*; *Canossa* stratagem*.

You play the "quarry" or the "victim," knowing full well that "quarries" and "victims" automatically attract sympathy. By virtue of self-abasement, self-weakening, self-prejudice, and so on, the stratagem user arouses some emotions, especially trust. In business life, this stratagem can also be used as an exploitation stratagem, and in this respect is a hybrid.

Stratagem radius

Politics: One day after an attempt was apparently made on his life, the Taiwanese president, Chen Shuibian, who was running for a second term, was reelected on March 20, 2004, with an extremely narrow majority of 0.2% of the votes cast (a lead of 30,000 votes).

---

*Translators' note: a reference to an Italian castle, where the Holy Roman Emperor, Henry IV, famously did penance in 1077 (*Stratageme 2*, pp. 692 ff).

The rival candidates of the Kuomintang (Chinese nationalist party) were allotted 49.9% of the vote. The attempted assassination caused an insignificant injury to Chen Shuibian, and was characterized by various inconsistencies. Inasmuch as events that seem strange to the Chinese are more or less automatically looked at from the point of view of stratagems, it was not surprising that, only six days later on the Chinese-speaking Internet, the search string "Chen Shuibian— the stratagem of the suffering flesh" had over 1,000 matches. On the other hand, as far as we know, it did not occur to a single Western commentator to look from the stratagem standpoint at the assassination attempt, which presumably earned Chen Shuibian the deciding winning votes. On the contrary, Western mouthpieces reported mockingly on "ludicrous conspiracy theories" in Taiwan (*NZZ*, April 2, 2004, p. 7).

Insurance business: A Japanese insurance company hired a large number of widows and trained them as insurance agents. By virtue of their employment, the company made enormous profits. Above all, the widows induced many married women to persuade their husbands to take out life insurance. For the widows, who traveled from house to house, were able to draw on their own ill fate: "If my husband had taken out a life-insurance policy, I wouldn't now have to live from hand to mouth as a hawker" (Yu 1994, pp. 286–7).

Sales: In China, sales are often advertised under signs such as "Great clearing-out sale" or "Opportunity to bleed us dry," which signal that great harm is being inflicted to the business. In this context, there's at least a faint correlation between the Chinese business maxim "Smaller profit, greater turnover" (*Bo li duo xiao*) and stratagem 34.

Educational system: An institute of science and technology reported that it presented a "ring of shame" to every graduate. A former student of this institute received a commission for a bridge-construction project, and, as a result of insufficient planning on his part, the bridge collapsed not long after its inauguration. After that, the institute bought some of the steel with which the bridge had been built, and produced a collection of rings from it. The graduates of the institute were supposed to wear the "ring of shame" on their fingers, as a daily reminder of the bridge fiasco and as a warning to be vigilant with regard to their own work.

Stratagem prevention

Sensitized by this stratagem, you should be bold enough to be vigilant against people who pose as victims and quarries, and against your own Samaritan instinct towards such people, in order not to allow pseudovictims and pseudoquarries to twist you around their little fingers; because "'victims' can be crafty fellows, too" (*NZZ*, February 9, 1996, p. 66). While you unmask false victims, you can and should support genuine victims and quarries with all your heart.

Stratagem risk

This stratagem is regarded as risky (Yu 1993, p. 372), because it doesn't work without some form of self-prejudice. For this reason you must keep a sense of proportion, and be very careful that any disadvantage is not irreversible.

Examples

Raining wristwatches

Stratagem 34 is used as a method of advertising, by letting a product publicly undergo the most thorough endurance tests, and then proving that no damage whatsoever has been suffered by it. In the spirit of stratagem 34, such endurance tests ensure that there is confidence in the quality of the product.

Thus, a Japanese watch company had a huge number of wristwatches, which were not yet market leaders, rain down from a helicopter from a height of 1,000 meters, and gave them away to the people who found them; all these people could confirm that the watches were in perfect working order, in spite of the impact (Chen 1, p. 346). Furthermore, the company had 1,000 wristwatches thrown into the sea with a propulsion device. After a while, a few dozen of them were propelled to the coast of the former Soviet Union, and even later washed up on the American coast. Again, the people who found them could confirm that all the watches were working perfectly, in spite of their long sea journey (Yao, pp. 161–2).

CEO salary: $1

As a management method, stratagem 34 is applied in the form of self-torment measures (self-imposed pay cuts; working to the point of exhaustion for all to see; implementation of a newly introduced harsh measure, first with respect to oneself; and so on). In this way, you make an example of yourself (Chen 1, p. 346). In 1979, when Lee Iacocca took over the Chrysler group, which was on the brink of ruin, and introduced rigid economy measures, he reduced his own salary to the symbolic level of $1 (*CM*, p. 1323). This self-imposed agony can be transformed into the quality of one's products, and one's individual suffering into the fighting spirit of one's subordinates, who can be motivated in this way. But managers' salaries that are perceived to be extremely high are the absolute opposite of this management method, and are very likely to cause ill feeling among subordinates, as well as in wide sections of the population. The leader who demands that others should tighten their belts should not line his own pockets, from the perspective of this stratagem. If the elite, who hold the purse strings, do not allow others to have a share in their success, then "there's a danger that they will forcefully take what is their due. We can see this at demonstrations against globalization" (*C*, March 25, 2004, p. 41).

The lost game of chance

Chinese businesspeople deliberately lose a game of mah-jongg, for example, and possibly lose money, with the intention of creating a pleasant atmosphere for their game partner, who is also their business partner.

The Opium War and unequal contracts

In the People's Republic of China, Western foreigners are confronted with the humiliations—even though often quite discreet, but no less effective—that the West has inflicted on China since the nineteenth century: whether it be the Opium War (1839–1842) between Britain and China; the pillage of the emperor's palace in Beijing by European troops a few years later; unequal contracts, through which Western powers won privileges in China; or many other facts, by means of which China can make itself out to be the victim of foreign aggression. The Chinese can also try to flag up this "victim bonus," at least behind the scenes, as regards business-contract negotiations with Western companies. When during negotiations Chinese representatives point to China as a poor, backward developing country, from which you must not demand high prices, one is reminded of stratagem 34 (Fang, p. 275; Brahm, p. 68).

Disclosure stratagems

A reality or a statement, which is unknown or difficult to communicate, is cleverly established or conveyed: stratagems 13, 26.

Stratagem 13:
Beating the grass to startle the snakes

The stratagem is aimed at obtaining and disseminating information, specifically in three respects.

1. Snakes are "startled" by vibrations, produced by a thud on the ground; they move away, thus making the grass rustle and betraying their presence. So the stratagem user quickly and conveniently knows that snakes—possibly poisonous ones—are hiding in the field in front of him, and he can be on his guard (Chen 2, p. 134).
   Sounding-balloon stratagem; test-run stratagem.

2. As far as the "snakes" are concerned, they are warned by means of the stratagem. By not beating the snakes directly, but the grass, someone is demonstrating that they will catch and kill the snakes, if the snakes themselves don't clear off of their own accord. "Killing a chicken to scare the monkey."
   Indirect-deterrent stratagem; warning-shot stratagem.

3. From the "startling" of the snakes, which causes the grass to rustle and alerts the stratagem user to the danger, your thoughts turn to a third understanding of stratagem 13. Unusual signals are used, not to get hold of information that is difficult to access, but to produce a reaction which, from the viewpoint of the signal receiver, is spontaneous but which from the viewpoint of the stratagem user is a reaction deliberately induced by him: "Luring the snake out of its hole."
   Provocation stratagem.

Stratagem radius

Sounding-balloon stratagem

By means of carefully targeted articles in the press, you can test reactions. You can use some short remarks to irritate a business partner, so that they start talking. You can interrupt their flow of speech with a few provocative words, in order to find out about their real opinion from the way they react.

You can organize the spread of rumors during a negotiation, so that they reach the opponent's ears; leak certain inside information; divulge pseudosecrets; or suddenly exert pressure—all these tactics can be used to observe the reaction of the opponent. Also, by posing a series of well-formulated, purely hypothetical questions (for example, what is the purchase price when the amount of purchases is doubled?/if the duration of the contract is trebled?/if the guarantee figure is reduced?), you can sound out the opponent's situation (Yu 1994, p. 113).

In accordance with a fanciful interpretation of this stratagem, the following aspects may be interpreted thus: market events as "grass," the products made by an enterprise as "bamboo canes," and the market potential as "snakes." If you can thoroughly and quickly understand how to interpret the signals produced, by means of the various products, and make appropriate, strategic, and tactical management decisions, you'll be successful with your products (Yu 1994, p. 109).

Warning-shot stratagem

In the People's Republic of China, certain measures for combating crime are regarded as a legitimate application of this stratagem: "Execute one person as a deterrent to 100" (Yu 2003, p. 67).

The American oil magnate John Paul Getty (1892–1976) is supposed to have laid the foundations of his fortune with the help of stratagem 13. He hired a local bank employee to take his place at the auction of a plot of land, which was suspected to have oil beneath it. This scared off the other interested parties, who believed that the banker was negotiating for a large oil company. Unnerved, they pulled out. Thus, Getty was able to purchase the piece of land quite cheaply, and later sell it at a giant profit (Yao, pp. 103ff.).[20]

Provocation stratagem

Bertrand Russell (1872–1970) began a lecture at Beijing University with the question "What does 2 + 2 make?" The lecture hall, which just a moment earlier had been noisy, became as quiet as a mouse. Nobody dared speak, because they suspected a trap. Then Russell gave the answer "2 + 2 = 4." And he continued, "Even elementary schoolchildren know that. You are all university students. Why couldn't you answer this question?" And then he launched into his lecture, in front of a captive audience, once he had shaken them out of their initial lethargy (Yu 2003, pp. 67–8).

During a *job interview* in China, "the grass is beaten to startle the snakes" with the intention of quickly ascertaining the mental agility of job applicants. For example, they are given a cake in a box. Then, they are set the task of cutting the cake into eight pieces and distributing them to eight people, but on the condition that one piece remains in the cake box. In the face of this strange task, many applicants racked their brains, without managing to find a solution. They failed. But there are other applicants who quickly grasp the solution. First, they distribute one piece of cake per person to seven of the eight people. Then, they put the eighth piece back in the box and give this to the eighth person. These applicants, who showed their imaginativeness, passed the test (*ZQB*, December 11, 2002, p. 12).

In *advertising*, you can "gain the upper hand and leave behind the brand message, through the cunning use of provocation and surprise" (*Der Spiegel*, no. 26, 2001, p. 70). But provocation can also be counterproductive and repugnant. That's why perceptiveness is indispensable here.

In the middle of a *negotiation*, you can gather up your documents and storm out of the negotiating room—which is another way to use provocation stratagem 13.

Stratagem prevention

If you ascertain that the negotiations are artificial and are only being used to extract as much information as possible, you should break off negotiations immediately. Confronted with a barrage of questions, you answer only those questions where you can show your greatest strengths and drive your opponent in the direction of your choice. On no account allow yourself to be cross-examined. Be careful with "What if …?" questions!

If you succumb to an emotional outburst because of the other party's action, to which you feel pressurized to give an instant reaction, you should immediately ask yourself whether this conforms precisely to a possible calculation of the other party, and whether the other party can exploit it to their advantage. If you answer in the affirmative to either of these questions, then fail to react. Don't let yourself be provoked! Recognize leading questions!

Stratagem risk

The sounding balloon you launch must be well conceived, otherwise the outcome is worthless. Sounding balloons released in a chaotic manner accomplish nothing. Let sleeping dogs lie!

If you trial a useless idea at an inopportune moment or in an amateurish fashion, to see how the land lies, the target groups could be provoked to unexpectedly harsh counter-reactions, which damage you.

Examples

Sounding-balloon stratagem: The informative price scare

A foreign businessman wanted to buy flavoring substances in China. He offered $40 per kilo in the transaction. The Chinese didn't know where they stood, and demanded $48. Startled, the foreign businessman shook his head and stammered, "No, no, that's much too expensive. There's no way that I can pay any more than $45 a kilo." So, he had involuntarily blurted out his uppermost limit, due to his irritation at the high price demanded by the Chinese. Of course, the transaction was concluded at $45 per kilo, and therefore at a higher price than the Chinese had initially hoped for (Yu 1994, p. 113).

Warning-shot stratagem: Only 40 minutes for dinner

The Chinese company A is discussing a joint venture with the German company B in China. They have only three days available for the discussions, and there are many areas of dispute. The negotiations proceed tenaciously. When the three men from the German delegation arrive at the evening banquet scheduled for eight o'clock, they are informed that the head of the Chinese negotiating delegation has sent apologies for his absence. The reason given is that he has to care for his sick father. At the news of the absence of the Chinese negotiating leader, the German delegates react by informing the baffled low-ranking Chinese who are present that they have only 40 minutes available for the evening meal. Afterwards, they must be back in their hotel room for important telephone calls with the German parent company. The Germans did indeed say their farewells after exactly 40 minutes, before the main course had even arrived.[21]

The head of the Chinese delegation tried to use stratagem 13. By making a clearly lame apology to gloss over his absence, he wanted to signal indirectly to the German side his disapproval of the previous sale negotiations, and to intimidate them. Only if they are more accommodating in future negotiations will he devote his time to them again, and also want to eat and drink with them; that was probably how the message was supposed to sound. Likewise, the Germans reacted spontaneously in accordance with the stratagem. With their effective banquet boycott, they wrecked the Chinese stratagem. Likewise, by using stratagem 13, the Germans simply slapped the Chinese back in the face. From the following day onward, the head of the Chinese delegation is said to have behaved in a more conciliatory fashion. He had noticed that the Germans were not dumb.

The fact that in this case the German side also—and, indeed, in a masterly fashion—negotiated according to the stratagem, and within the framework of a defensive reaction, only confirms the theory that cunning behavior is universal. Mind you, I don't suppose the Germans recognized which stratagem they were using in response to which stratagem.

Provocation stratagem: Enjoyment of wine by virtue of a smashed bottle

At the second world wine-tasting convention, the various Chinese wines went unnoticed because of their dull external presentation, although the wines themselves were of good quality. Then stratagem 13 occurred to a member of the Chinese wine delegation, and he implemented it straightaway. There was a shattering sound—and a bottle of Maotai lay on the floor, in pieces. Immediately, a beguiling aroma wafted up and spread across the whole room. Wine connoisseurs from all over the world rushed over and exclaimed, "What a fine wine!" Thereafter, the spell on Chinese wines was broken (Chen 2, p. 136).

Stratagem 26:
Cursing the acacia, [while] pointing at the mulberry tree

指
桑
罵
槐

For all to see, you revile the common "mulberry tree," whose leaves are used by farmers as food for silkworms, but, in reality, you are referring to the acacia next to it, which is much nobler and therefore not so easily open to attack. "Kick the dog and mean the master." Depending on the circumstances, the stratagem user's objective can be to draw the attention only of those surrounding the "acacia" to the indirect criticism of it. But the objective can also be for the "acacia" itself to take note of the indirect criticism inflicted upon it, and to take it to heart. Especially in delicate negotiations, you cannot always bluntly tell your opponent negative things to their face, especially if they are powerful. Then, stratagem 26 can be helpful. Criticism of the "mulberry tree" should be precisely administered with regard to the envisaged goal, the "acacia"; it should not be confusing, but comprehensible, so that the "acacia," albeit in a subtle way, feels really concerned, but not offended or provoked. The stratagem must by no means always be directed at a person. It can also be used for criticism of an object. So you can give expression to your indignation about an entire project by condemning a detail of it.

Indirect-criticism stratagem; shadowboxing stratagem.

Shoot at silhouette targets (cut-out dummies of the human form); criticize a small or personal flaw in the opponent, thereby indirectly calling into question their strengths or professional competence, too (Yan, p. 74); attack a weak enemy and—of course—defeat them, to induce a stronger enemy to yield.

Indirect-aggression stratagem.

Stratagem radius

After America's war against Iraq (March–April 2003), the Libyan head of state, Colonel Gaddafi, suddenly announced his intention to give up his weapons of mass destruction and bring about a rapprochement with America. The former CIA director James Woolsey expressed his opinion on the effect of stratagem 26, which was a reflection of the outcome of the Iraq war: "The fact that Gaddafi eventually decided to be upfront about his activities is, undoubtedly, to do with the American—British action against Iraq. Those who still believe that Libya in any way had a change of heart are most likely to be naive" (*NZZ*, March 13/14, 2004, p. 7).

Several of Jesus' parables in the New Testament can be interpreted as applications of stratagem 26, for example, the one about the wicked tenants (Mark 12:1–12). And in the television series *Star Trek: The Next Generation*, behind the unstoppable, expanding intergalactic villains, the Borg, who assimilate or annihilate everything in their path, many see a clear allusion to the immensely powerful earthly group Microsoft (*C*, August 2, 2002, p. 31).

Stratagem prevention

A weak person should not expose himself to such an extent that he has to play the role of a "mulberry tree." There are situations in which you must stand by the "mulberry tree," which is directly the object of an attack, to prevent yourself being designated as the next "mulberry tree." If you become concerned about your role as the "mulberry tree," you can immediately pass on criticism if need be, or ignore it, relying on stratagem 27, "Feigning madness without losing the balance."

Stratagem risk

The indirect attack, which should only be perceived by those around the "acacia" and not by the "acacia" itself, contrary to expectations, doesn't escape the attention of the "acacia," which will take bitter revenge. Indirect criticism, which above all the "acacia" should take note of, is not perceived by it, because the "mulberry tree," which is directly criticized, shows no parallels to the "acacia" whatsoever. Therefore, the "acacia" believes that criticism was really for the "mulberry tree."

Example

Fury at the waiter

During negotiations, you can feign an outburst of rage against a disinterested person, for example, a waiter, in order to illustrate to the negotiating partner your total frustration. Or you can tear up the draft contract, your face contorted with anger, to make your opponent graphically aware of the tense situation (Yu 1994, p. 216). In advertising campaigns, you can criticize your competitors without mentioning their names, but in such a way that the consumers know their identity (Li, pp. 301–2).

Exploitation stratagems

The quick-witted exploitation of a favorable situation which the opponent fails to notice—due to poor mental alertness, missing information, scanty knowledge, or lack of imagination—or which he is unable to influence: stratagems 2, 4, 5, 12, 14, 15, 16, 17, 18, 19, 20, 22, 23, 28, 30, 31, 33.

Stratagem 2:

Besieging [the undefended capital of the country of] Wei to rescue Zhao [the country that has been attacked by the Wei forces]

Indirect conquest of the opponent by threatening one of its unprotected weak points. It involves penetrating into the "empty" and avoiding the "full." "Empty" stands for positions in which the opponent is ill-prepared or totally unprepared; "full" stands for the opposite scenario.

Achilles-heel stratagem.

In accordance with a generalization of the meaning of stratagem 2, you can begin to solve certain problems arising from a comparatively light-hearted secondary aspect. If there is a successful breakthrough here, it can spur on your own people and produce a faster solution to the overall problem.

Stratagem radius

The emergence of the information society makes companies and states vulnerable. Private individuals and small groups can carry out attacks using the Internet, which is economical and effective (*HBM*, November 2003, p. 77). Worldwide, ships' captains, car drivers, amateur sportspeople, and others, who want to know their location down to the last meter, use the satellite-protected Global Positioning System (GPS). However, GPS satellite signals can be scrambled by jamming transmitters. Optical sensors can be dazzled with lasers; satellites can be destroyed by letting them collide with combat satellites. It is not necessarily the side that has the high technology that is powerful, but the side that understands the system, can circumvent it, and knows how to radically exploit its weaknesses. It's no wonder that the American defense secretary warned of a new

"Pearl Harbor." America may be threatened, "because their base in outer space could be brought to a standstill" (*Die Zeit*, February 22, 2001, p. 5; *Der Spiegel*, no. 38, 2001, p. 245).

You tackle a sore point in the position or personality of the opponent during negotiations (Fang, p. 263).

Stratagem prevention

You must know and protect your weak points.

Stratagem risk

You can misjudge your opponent's weak points, and then bang your head against a brick wall.

Example

After the outbreak of World War I, western European exports to China fell off considerably. Above all, the Chinese soap market suffered as a result. Fan Xudong, a Chinese chemist and entrepreneur, seized the opportunity that presented itself with both hands. In 1918, he founded China's first manufacturing venture in soap products, by the name of *Yongli* ("Endless Profit"). Yet after the end of World War I, the British company Bruner, Mond & Co., which had dominated the Chinese soap market before the outbreak of war, forced its way back into this market with all its might. Of course, it was bothered by the newly emerged Chinese rival, and it did everything in its power to bring it under control—but in vain. Eventually, the British company dumped an enormous quantity of soap onto the Chinese market, at a 40% price reduction. This move hit the Yongli company very hard. Undercutting the competition's price was ruled out, because bankruptcy would inevitably follow. But, of course, it could not dispose of the more expensive soap either, and therefore takings failed to materialize. On no account did

Fan Xudong want to capitulate to the British. One day, he went into his study, where he paced up and down with head bowed, to devise a countermeasure. Then, suddenly, his eye fell on a picture hanging on the wall. It was a picture of him in Japan, where he had studied. Japan! That was the solution. Japan was Bruner's most important market in the Far East. Europe was still weakened from World War I, and that was why Bruner's production volume was still limited and the company couldn't supply as much soap as it would have liked to the Far East. If Bruner now dumped such huge quantities of soap onto the market in China, the soap market Bruner supplied in Japan would be overstretched. So why not attack the Bruner company— which had launched a frontal attack on him in China—in a roundabout way via Japan?

At that time, the two Japanese groups Mitsubishi and Mitsui were in fierce competition for domination of the Japanese market. Mitsubishi owned a soap factory, but Mitsui didn't possess such an enterprise. If it wanted to sell soap, too, it had to rely on imports. Was this not the place for a business breakthrough? Hastily, Fan Xudong contacted Mitsui, and proposed to the group that it take over the sales of "Red Triangle," the soap made by Yongli, at a lower price than Bruner's in Japan. They swiftly reached an agreement. Overnight, Red Triangle soap was distributed throughout Japan by the giant sales network of the Mitsui group. Equal in quality to the Bruner soap, the more economical Chinese soap caused a dramatic reduction in the price of soap throughout Japan. So Bruner had to follow suit with price-cutting. As sales of Bruner soap in Japan were greater by far than in China, the price cuts led to heavy losses. Its Chinese soap sales accounted for only about one-tenth of Bruner's soap sales. Moreover, the retail price in Japan was somewhat higher than the lowest Bruner soap price in China. Therefore, losses for Fan Xudong were comparatively insignificant. Consequently, Bruner in fact had the upper hand in China, but found itself in an undesirable situation in Japan, which was more important to it. Bruner recognized that it could not fight on two fronts simultaneously. It came to the conclusion that protecting its market in Japan was more important than its attack on Fan Xudong in China. That's why Bruner signaled to Fan Xudong, not long after Xudong's entry into the Japanese market, that it wanted to stop selling soap at giveaway prices in China, and hoped in return that Fan Xudong would cease his activities in Japan. Fan Xudong made use of this opportunity and demanded that, for the rest, if Bruner wanted to alter the price of soap on the Chinese market, it would have to obtain his consent beforehand. All Bruner could do was agree.

A writer on Chinese stratagems concludes: The powerful company Bruner had wielded the scepter over the Chinese market in an arrogant way for a time, and had mistakenly believed that the fledgling Yongli would collapse under the first blow. Yet its deadly offensive was completely shot down by Fan Xudong, thanks to skillful use of the stratagem "Besieging Wei to rescue Zhao." Every opponent, no matter how strong, definitely has an area where he is comparatively weak; the central idea behind "Besieging Wei to rescue Zhao" is to avoid direct confrontation with the opponent and attack him where he is weak (Wei 1992).

Stratagem 4:
Awaiting at one's ease the exhausted enemy

Sitting-it-out stratagem; exhaustion stratagem.

If you understand something about the conduct of war, you "control the enemy and don't let yourself be controlled by them," as it is said in Master Sun's *The Art of War*. That's why you try to behave like the hedgehog in Grimm's fairy tale of the hare and the hedgehog: You're one step ahead and, in top form, you play your game with your exhausted opponent.

"Don't risk being the first under heaven," advised

the legendary Chinese philosopher Lao-tzu (who reputedly flourished in the seventh century BC). In this sense, as far as economic competition is concerned, the use of stratagem 4 with regard to risky new products can involve relinquishing the lead to the competitor and only "taking the offensive after the other side has fired the first shot" (*hou fa zhi ren*). While the competitor struggles with the launching and marketing of their new product, you can analyze this calmly, examining and utilizing the positive and negative reactions of the public. In future, you can develop a more refined alternative product, and trump your opponent with it. (Yu 1994, pp. 31, 35).

With interpersonal problems, sitting it out may lead to their resolution in the course of time (Chen 2, p. 39).

Stratagem radius

In a letter to me dated May 10, 1989, the then chancellor of Germany *Helmut Kohl* made the following comments about this stratagem: "For politicians, stratagem 4 'Awaiting at one's ease the exhausted enemy' seems to me particularly worthy of consideration, if it simultaneously follows the warning you quoted by the philosopher Hong Zicheng: 'You must not have a heart that harms people! But a heart that is wary of people is indispensable!'"

An American allegedly complained that Saudi Arabia's former oil minister and OPEC president Sheikh Yamani very successfully tired out members of the audience at *conferences*, as he spoke with quite a low voice and repeated himself ad nauseam (Yu 1994, p. 30).

Generally, the Chinese use patience against Western impatience during *negotiations*. Furthermore, as a rule, they proceed more on the basis of time-consuming rounds of negotiation, and possibly also on the basis of lengthy individual meetings, than their Western partners do. During negotiations in China, time and again evening entertainment programs are slipped in, which drag on late into the night, and can contribute to the exhaustion of the Western partner. Chinese negotiating delegations often include many more members than foreign delegations do, and therefore have at their disposal more replacements in their staff-rotation system at the negotiating table (Fang, p. 264).

Stratagem prevention

When you push ahead enthusiastically, and put your heart and soul into specific ventures, playing for the highest stakes, do not forget the Chinese proverb "The praying mantis catches the cicada, but the titmouse is already lurking behind." Small businesses in particular should always take into consideration the fact that while they're making a genuine effort, a powerful competitor is calmly awaiting his opportunity.

Stratagem risk

Waiting must not degenerate into missed opportunities.

Example

The latecomer reaps the rewards

In the fifties, the Japanese company Matsushita moved belatedly into the Japanese electronics market in a race to catch up, by flooding the market with considerably optimized television sets and tape recorders, in comparison with rival products (Lin, p. 36). Similarly, between 1970 and 1980, comparatively smaller, energy-saving, and more comfortable Japanese cars won a considerable share of the world market, too, although they didn't appear until quite late on the world market. Indeed, a large proportion of Japanese economic success might be founded on the advantage the Japanese gained from the fact that Western countries had been bringing their technical products onto the market over a long period. Now the

Japanese could buckle down; copy and improve these products, giving them a new finish; and then overwhelm the Western product forerunners with their attractive, imitation-perfect goods. In the People's Republic of China, these Japanese procedures are regarded as exemplary, in both domestic and international markets (Yu 1994, p. 83).

Stratagem 5:
Taking advantage of a conflagration to commit robbery

Taking advantage of another's predicament, difficulties, crisis, and ignorance.

Vulture stratagem; exploitation-of-plight stratagem.

It's worth discovering shortcomings and dangers, the rectification of which can earn you money. You can make a virtue out of necessity and an opportunity out of a crisis. Even the negative often has a positive side. Reappraise the negative in a positive way! With a past mistake, find tips for a possible future solution! Turn a defeat around into a burst of energy! Extract the positive side from a depressing piece of news! Convert resistance to self-motivation! Find strength in adversity! Perceive a disaster as an incentive, let a debacle become a stroke of luck! Managers who land up in jail can take a leaf out of actor Ernst Hannawald's book. He was sentenced to five years' imprisonment for carrying out two bank raids while under the influence of drugs in 1997. In the spirit of stratagem 5, he commented, "Prison saved my life" (*Blick*, Zurich, March 27, 2002, p. 25).

Stratagem radius

Worldwide, there are "looting knights," who gain from the difficult position of other market competitors or make a profit from any catastrophe (Yu 1994, pp. 37, 39–40). When the American Civil War broke out in 1861, J. P. Morgan (1837–1913) regarded "this not as a catastrophe, but as a business opportunity" (Yao, pp. 36ff.). The American meat magnate Philip Danforth Armour (1832–1901) found out about the outbreak of an epidemic in Mexico by reading an inconspicuous item in the newspaper, thus displaying a habit of close reading that would be commended in the People's Republic of China. He immediately concluded that the meat supply affected by the epidemic, from the American states bordering Mexico—at that time, these states were the most important meat-producing area in America—would decline, and the price of meat would rise suddenly. Without delay, Armour took out credit, bought up all the supplies of beef and pork he could get hold of from the American states bordering Mexico, and transported them to the eastern states of America, where he stored them. A little later, the epidemic really took hold in the American states bordering Mexico. The price of meat rose enormously. Then, Armour flooded the market with his stockpiled meat—and made a giant profit (Zhang, pp. 56–7).

When the oil crises shook the world in the seventies, Japanese car manufacturers "took advantage of a conflagration to commit robbery," achieving massive sales with energy-saving small cars at home and abroad (Chen 1, pp. 211ff.; Chen 2, p. 53).

In Germany, the *poverty business* is booming. "More and more citizens, who are heavily in debt, land in the clutches of loan sharks and unscrupulous debt advisers" (*Die Welt*, June 6, 2003, p. 21). Similar profiteering is also lamented in the People's Republic of China (*ZQB*, December 12, 2002, p. 1, and January 6, 2003, p. 7).

In their book *Silence, on tue* (Paris 1986), André Glucksmann and Thierry Wolton claim, "There are *catastrophe profiteers*, who'd rather keep quiet, in order to preserve their image or so as not to unnerve contributors. Hunger is their job; they are commercial travelers in matters of hunger."[22]

People traffickers drag illegal workers to Europe where they are exploited as the very cheapest labor (*NZZ*, February 2, 2004, p. 30).

These people leave their homes, because they are already in need or dissatisfied with their economic situation there. In Europe, they are in even more of a predicament, as they find themselves "without rights" here (*NZZ am Sonntag*, February 8, 2004, p. 2). So, to some extent, a double crisis experienced by these people is exploited.

Bad times are good for *astrologers*, *palmists*, and others who promise to satisfy metaphysical needs (*NZZ*, October 24, 2001, p. 61).

The Chinese profit from the difficult circumstances of Western companies, and buy them up at a good price (Yu 1993, p. 50). Chinese *negotiating partners* can exploit the ignorance of their foreign partners with regard to the Chinese market.

Stratagem prevention

If the "conflagration" is averted by preventative means, or if its flames are immediately extinguished, nobody can exploit it for "looting." Further, you must be careful that the conflagration doesn't originate in the "stratagem of the suffering flesh," serving as bait, through which the "looter," approaching in a careless manner, is apprehended.

Stratagem risk

The person who draws closer to the fire, in order to steal, can catch fire themselves and, during the looting, fall victim to the flames.

Examples

Wild East for Western gene researchers

For example, in the field of genome analyses, Western companies and institutes exploit China's incomplete laws and the ignorance of the population, above all in rural areas. Time and again, you read that China is a Wild East for gene researchers. On numerous occasions, blood has been taken from unsuspecting farmers. "Thus, the renowned Harvard University enticed farmers in the mountains of the remote province of Anhui with the promise that they would be treated for nothing (bait stratagem 17, 'Tossing out a brick to attract jade'). Instead of treatment, they received merely a bowl of instant noodles. Harvard claimed that the farmers had given their written agreement—admittedly, without understanding what they had agreed to, as was later shown. Moreover, many of the signatures subsequently turned out be forged" (*WW*, no. 14, 2004, pp. 60–1).

Rats in the rice

In Shanghai, a Soviet cargo ship was loading up sacks with rice, for export from China to the former Soviet Union. When half the ship was already crammed with sacks, a Soviet sailor suddenly cried out, "Rats!" Actually, three rats were peeking through one of the sacks. They were immediately killed. But then, the Soviet captain took the three dead rats and contacted the Chinese side. He demanded that the loading work cease straightaway. Thereupon he threw all the sacks that had already been loaded out of the ship. Further, he insisted that the Chinese side call in the World Health Organization. For fear of loss of face internationally, the Chinese side realized that they were forced to grin and bear it, and to pay the captain 100,000 Chinese dollars in compensation, so as to reassure him and at least be able to conclude the transaction. The three rats, according to a Chinese stratagem writer, were certainly no "conflagration," but the Soviet captain took advantage of this piece of bad luck, to pocket a healthy profit (Yu 1993, pp. 49–50).

Stratagem 12:

[Quick-wittedly] leading away the sheep [that unexpectedly crosses one's path]

Here, the "sheep" represents any surprising opportunity unrelated to your initial goals (Yuan, p. 142). Just picture a simple scene in ancient China. A farmer goes into a forest to gather some wood. As it happens, on his way, a stray sheep crosses his path. Showing cleverness and presence of mind, he takes the sheep with him. Were he less crafty, he would either not have noticed it, or have seen it and let it go on its way, since he would have been totally preoccupied with gathering wood. Stratagem 12 gives you the impulse, and mentally equips you to spot and to utilize any chance to gain an unexpected advantage.

Chances-to-gain stratagem; kairos *stratagem*; *serendipity stratagem.*

Kairos is an ancient Greek term for an unexpectedly favorable opportunity, such as occurs only once in a lifetime. The term "serendipity" is derived from the princes of Serendip, characters in an old fairy tale (*KdL*, pp. 171ff.). The princes would take note of the most apparently insignificant details, as if they were "sheep" crossing their paths, enabling them to gain an advantage later that could not have been predicted.

This stratagem draws on the "decisiveness toward the moment" (Martin Heidegger). You cannot always plan what will be crucial in life. Thus, it is of the utmost importance to be as alert as possible to unexpectedly favorable possibilities that turn up outside your main area of activity, so that you are aware of, and make the most of them. As the writer Nicholas Sparks puts it, "Good luck requires decisiveness—you must seize the opportunity as soon as it comes along."

As Voltaire has it, you should know that "Sometimes, by sheer coincidence, history creates an opening into the future," through which you can or rather, must go. As a politician, you must grasp the mantle of history. Listen attentively and stay wide awake, so that you can identify the starting points for attaining your negotiation targets as quickly as possible; and keep your wits about you, so that you can make the most of them. Remember: Every minute that passes is gone forever. Live in the "here and now" according to the maxim "I have no control over how long I live, but I can decide how effectively I use the time I am given." You must infer from this that each second could destroy all your dreams, goals, and visions; but it could also change everything for the better. Increase your awareness of the weight of each single moment. Learn to see when you are in the right place at the right time, meeting the right person. It is not enough to have a good idea: You must carry it out. Sometimes you must be ruthless, and use the opportunity to take painful measures. If the chance arises, you must even steal someone else's show. Stay awake, and always evaluate the situation accurately. You must not be daydreaming when the situation changes. You must have a keen nose for potentially profitable trends. In addition, you must always find out about the latest developments, then quickly turn them into profitable schemes or products. Never limit your scope: Always look out for gaps and unfilled niches in the market, and fill them. Make the most of your competitors' omissions, as well as of your own scientific and technological advantages. Never underestimate any advantage, however apparently unimportant—even if it barely seems worth mentioning. Even in the quietest moments the seeds of an important development may be present, either for better or for worse. You should calmly seize the new shoots of the future, then either go along with it, or, if it is heading in the wrong direction, nip it in the bud. Finally, never forget to enjoy your achievements.

Stratagem radius

On a small piece of cheese that had accidentally fallen into a bacteria culture, Alexander Fleming (1881–1955) discovered a blue-green mold that was white around the edges. A less observant researcher would have missed this. He then isolated the area of mold and identified it as penicillin. For this discovery, Alexander Fleming received the Nobel Prize in 1945. Viagra was also discovered largely by chance. Walter Köbele, head of Pfizer in Germany, recalls: "Originally, we were researching drugs to prevent the constriction of blood vessels. Then we noticed a remarkable side effect on the male volunteers in our trials: better erections when they were aroused. Soon after this, we conducted studies to identify the active ingredient. Viagra was the result of this, and is now one of our top ten products" (*mobil*, no. 3, 2004, p. 41).

Chinese firms are particularly adept at filling market niches. They notice areas of the market that Western market leaders have abandoned, or that do not interest them, because they reckon their likely profits to be too low. Since their production costs are minimal, these Chinese firms make large profits in areas where their Western competitors gained nothing. With their convenient and—especially—cheap products, they even manage to meet the needs of Western consumers. In so doing, "they astound their Western competitors" (*HBR*, October 2003, p. 95), who set greater store by high-tech business. Take Huawei, for example, which entered the world market with comparatively simple routers that cost 40% less than its competitors' more advanced products. By 2002, it already accounted for 3% of the world market. Or take Haier, which, by the early nineties, had already overtaken Whirlpool, Electrolux, Siemens, and Matsushita in the Chinese market for domestic appliances. In 1994, it entered the American market, and concentrated for five years on producing refrigerators with a capacity of less than 180 liters, which could be used in minibars, or by students with little space in their rooms. American market leaders had regarded this area of the market as unimportant, yet it proved very profitable for Haier. Of course, the Chinese were by no means the first to use this stratagem. After World War II, the secret of Japanese commercial success was to move into Western markets with small, cheap, and convenient appliances (Lin, p. 94). These included pocket transistor radios, portable cassette recorders (or "Walkmans"), television sets, hand-held video cameras, and Honda scooters. Western companies considered such products trivial.

French trade unions are fond of using major events to make their demands, since they know that the government wants to avoid any conflict, if possible, and will generally give in. Thus, before the 1998 World Cup, pilots from Air France and railroad workers from the SNCF (Société nationale des chemins de fer français) went on strike (*Süddeutsche Zeitung*, November 30, 2001, p. 5).

Some *banks* are accused of massively overcharging their credit-card customers, charging excessive annual fees to credit-card holders, and charging horrendous interest rates on existing debts, and, in addition, they demand commissions that traders, and bar and hotel managers, have to pay (*Blick*, Zurich, January 22, 2002, p. 1; *Saldo*, Zurich, no. 1, 2004, p. 19).

Managers with the "rip-off mentality" (*BZ*, March 26, 2004, p. 18) are "crafty exploiters" of weaknesses in the market-economy system. They use tactics rather than achievements to get high-ranking posts, and, as soon as they have got there, they hire advisers to do the work for them.

Language itself can be skillfully exploited. For example, according to Swiss pharmaceutical law, it is forbidden to sell so-called "zappers" (or energy providers), electrical devices that supposedly protect against all serious illnesses, even anthrax. Hence, a mail-order specialist bookseller does not "sell" them, but "provide" them to the Swiss market. Firms officially "sell" them in Germany and Poland (*TA*, October 30, 2001).

Stratagem 12 can be implemented destructively through the (mis)use of power.

Stratagem prevention

You must not give anyone the opportunity to use this stratagem against you. Never leave any baggage unattended in airports or railroad stations! Never show any weaknesses: You should always think before you act or speak, to consider whether your actions or words leave you vulnerable to bullying or harassment.

Legislators should not make laws full of loopholes that can be cleverly exploited. For example, financial markets should never make it easy for terrorists to finance their criminal activities. Technical devices should be tested to see how vulnerable they are to stratagems. For instance, a fingerprint system can be "fooled" using a commonplace soft candy, and you can trick a sensor using an adhesive (*NZZ*, July 2, 2002, p. 11; *Handelsblatt*, June 7/8, 2002, p. 21).

Stratagem risk

Without sound knowledge and judgment, there is the danger that you will catch a "sick sheep," or take a chance that brings you no reward.

Examples

A Bavarian official's unguarded comment

In June 1980, Jiang Nanxiang, the Chinese minister of education, and a number of delegates visited West Germany. They spent one rather unspectacular day in Munich, where they went sightseeing. At their farewell dinner that evening, Dr. Karl Böck, the head of a department in the Bavarian Ministry of Culture, was seated next to Jiang Nanxiang. The meal was a very quiet affair, until Dr. Böck asked the Chinese minister a few questions, so that he did not appear rude: "So, Minister, what is your impression of Germany so far? Has it given you any ideas? Are there any people you wish to meet, or places you wish to visit?" The minister had been quiet and withdrawn all evening, but was suddenly wide awake. He explained that the so-called Cultural Revolution (1966–1976) had severely impaired Chinese education. "*Before I'd really given it any thought,*" recounts Dr. Böck, "my answer just came out." He conceded that a one-week visit was too short for the minister to be able to answer his questions, and went on, "Let me make a suggestion. If you would like to find out if working with Germany could help you in this area, just send two German-speaking experts here, to the Bavarian Ministry of Education, for six months. They can read, see, and ask anything; take part in any meetings; and make any contacts that they consider worth while. Then, after six months, they can tell you whether there is any basis for Sino-German cooperation concerning matters of education." Dr. Böck recalls, "This was really just meant to be a consolation for a disappointed guest. *But it was more than that.* In his after-dinner speech, Jiang Nanxiang said that he was deeply impressed by what the Germans had achieved, but that what he had seen showed him how much catching up his own country had to do. Until now, nothing had really given him any idea as to what to do about his problems back home. *The first useful suggestion he had received had come from the man sitting next to him, and, if it was meant sincerely, he would very much like to take him up on his offer.* Though I was happy that he had accepted my offer, I was also worried about how it would look. But I had given my word, so we had to go through with it" (Karl Böck, *Süddeutsche Zeitung*, November 23/24, 1985, p. 141).

The German had made a suggestion without really thinking about it, more as a consolation than anything else. It was the "sheep" that suddenly crossed the Chinese minister's path. Until then, he had seemed inattentive, but he was alert to every possibility. Resolutely and without hesitation, he led the "sheep" away with him. Because of this, the Bavarians and the Chinese worked together for many years, which was a very fruitful development for the Chinese educational system.

Luckless in Germany, but a market leader in Japan

The German "Transrapid" is one of the best and safest forms of transportation in the world. It took more than two decades to develop before actually transporting passengers—in China. In a similar vein, a German writes, "We went to sleep and missed out on all the most important products: PlayStations, laptops, laser printers, digital cameras—all made in Japan, America, Taiwan, Singapore, or Malaysia" (*B*, April 5, 2004, p. 9). But whenever there is a political debate about how Germany's failed technology policies have led to its current economic crisis, the fax machine is always cited as the prime example. Some even call this the "German trauma" (*Berner Zeitung*, September 6, 2002).[23] For German inventors played a decisive role in the development of the fax machine, but it was made commercially viable by the Japanese and the Americans.

Rudolf Hell (1901–2002) invented the *Hell-Schreiber* in 1929. This was the direct forerunner of the fax machine, but, at this stage, *no one even thought about mass-producing it*.[24] Instead of printing dots and dashes like a Morse-code machine, the *Hell-Schreiber* receiver would actually print out fully formed words. Hell sold the patent for his machine to Siemens in 1929, and, in 1931, Siemens put his machine into production and marketed it. After World War II, in his Kiel-based two-man firm, Hell successfully developed the first machine to send pictures, which laid the foundations for the modern-day fax machine. This development was possible because Siemens had decided not to go into picture telegraphy. So, when it came to developing picture-sending devices, Hell was on his own. In 1956, he unveiled the first fax machine, called KF 108,[25] and even invented the first fax machines for office use in 1971.[26] Thus, the fax machine was invented in Schleswig-Holstein. But it was first mass-produced outside Germany. The Japanese particularly liked the idea of fax technology: It would allow them to send complex messages in pictograms around the world, and thus open up new markets. Consequently, they developed the technology further, and the fax machine finally got its international breakthrough. Within a few years, every business had an inexpensive and convenient Japanese fax machine, and a few years after that, many households also had one. Nowadays, fax technology already appears dated: Email is faster and more practical, because you can send your original documents, and your addressees can print them out for themselves. But the fax machine is tough and will survive: It is a reassuring pillar of the modern world of communications (*Berner Zeitung*, September 6, 2002).[27]

"What measures did this government take to promote a technology transfer between universities, and information and communication businesses? Were advisers placed in universities? Were patenting agencies set up? And how are these to be evaluated, given that the fax machine was invented in Schleswig-Holstein, but was first mass-produced elsewhere?" These questions were put to the government of Schleswig-Holstein by the SDP (Social Democratic Party) representatives.[28] The questions, however, are misguided, since the fax machine was invented not in a university, but by a firm. The inventor was not a university academic without any business acumen, but a German entrepreneur with decades of commercial experience. He simply did not market his product well enough. Nevertheless, the government of Schleswig-Holstein failed to answer the question about how they could avoid missing opportunities again, the way they had missed out on the fax machine.[29] Did they lack a suitable intellectual approach to formulate an answer to this question?

Let us put this German failure in terms of stratagem 12. In the form of the fax machine that he had developed, a "sheep" crossed a German businessman's path, but he lacked the presence of mind to seize hold of it. By failing even to recognize the extent of its potential, let alone exploit it on a global scale, he missed the commercial chance that this "sheep" gave him. He invented a practical machine and failed to realize its market potential (Seitz, p. 329).[30] Why did no German manager know anything about Japanese script? The Germans could have marketed the fax machine successfully in Japan, as an indirect way of breaking into the international market. Sadly, the Germans are still failing to make the most of their own inventions. Look at Heiko Neupert, the inventor of malleable stone.[31] In April 2004, he won the Grand Prize in Geneva, at the 32nd International Inventors' Fair, yet in Germany his invention is virtually unknown, and though he has received a number of offers to commercialize his invention, they have mostly come from China.[32]

Maybe even now "sheep" are crossing German entrepreneurs' paths, only to be ignored for some reason or other—maybe political considerations, or just their failure to appreciate the "sheep's" potential worth. Consequently, they will end up in other countries. This may sound simplistic, but then, as René A. Frey, professor of national economics at the University of Basel, said in his farewell lecture, an economist must pluck up the courage to "represent complex facts in a simple way" (*NZZ*, March 31, 2004, p. 21).

"Germans look at the world either through a magnifying glass, or through a microscope. Thus, anything in their field of vision either appears too far away or too near." This quotation, from the erstwhile rector of the University of Beijing, Jiang Menglin (1886–1964), was reiterated by Lu Qiutian, Chinese ambassador to Germany from 1997 to 2001.[33] Neither a pair of binoculars nor a microscope can tell you about the path on which you are actually traveling. To bridge the gap with their international competitors, Germans should stop dreaming and fussing about trivialities, and should focus instead on the immediate and longer-term way ahead. Perhaps the 36 stratagems could help them think and act more tactically and strategically.

Stratagem 14:
Borrowing a corpse for the soul's return

This stratagem is formulated according to ancient teachings about reincarnation. Something old and worn is filled with new content. Thus, it appears old, but is not really.

Renovation stratagem; reheating stratagem; patina stratagem.

You are almost dead, but even in your miserable situation, you still have a "soul." You cannot drag yourself out of the mire using your own strength, so you could do with a "corpse," in which you could come back to life. You have suffered a terrible defeat, but you still have a sound mind and good judgment: You just need a helpful prop to rise again.

Phoenix stratagem; parasite stratagem.

Here, the "corpse" represents anything apparently useless. To apply stratagem 14, you must depend on something that seems to have no use. For example, a bird cannot fly without feathers. Although feathers are nothing special in themselves, and nothing useful can be done with them on their own, they enable birds to fly high, as well as far and wide. Thus, the apparently "useless" is useful. Stratagem 14 derives from this insight.

Even if you suffer a setback, you must never give up your "soul." As long as you keep your "soul," there is a chance that you may find a "corpse"—in other words, something that your competitors consider unviable or out of style—in which to return to life and make your comeback.

Stratagem radius

Sometimes, when establishing a new dynasty, the next in line from the previous dynasty is chosen as the ruler, in order to make the new dynasty appear legitimate. The Japanese adopted this approach in the 1930s, when they appointed the "last emperor of China." He was put in nominal charge of Manchuria, a state that they had founded, though the Japanese wielded the real power.

Christians have often used stratagem 14. In AD 354, for example, Pope Liberius declared that December 25—a feast day in the Roman Empire, since it was recognized as the birthday of Mithras, the Indo-Iranian god of light—was actually Jesus Christ's birthday (*Strategeme 1*, pp. 264–5). More recently, in Africa, missionaries often turned existing feasts and rituals into Christian solemnities. In addition, the earliest churches and monasteries were built as often as possible on existing sites of worship. In this way, they probably intended to drive out and replace existing customs and rituals with their new beliefs.

Stalin was a Marxist and an internationalist; hence, he opposed the idea of the nation state. Nevertheless, when Hitler invaded the Soviet Union in 1942, Stalin suddenly discovered a "corpse": patriotism. To rally his troops, he referred to their fight against the Nazis not as a "great proletarian war," but as a "great patriotic war." For he knew that nationalist rhetoric would be far more effective than Marxist arguments. More recently, President Putin ordered the Russian parliament to set the new text of the country's national anthem to the music of Stalin's old Soviet anthem. Stalin had introduced this anthem in 1944, but it was scrapped by Boris Yeltsin in 1991. Clearly, Putin wanted to inspire the Russians with nostalgic national pride, reminding them of the Soviet Union's victory over Germany in 1945, and of successful Soviet space exploration (*NZZ*, December 6, 2000, p. 5), by playing the old anthem. Thus, it would galvanize the new Russia.

In Singapore, cars must be withdrawn from the roads after ten years, though many of them are still roadworthy. So some car dealers export these "old" cars to countries like Indonesia, India, and Sri Lanka, thus imbuing them with new life (Wee, pp. 58–9).

As part of the Cultural Revolution (1966–1976) in China, all across the country, old cultural landmarks were destroyed. After the Cultural Revolution, however, thanks to old fables and legends, people in many regions of China discovered traces of their lost cultural heritage, and used it to make themselves interesting to tourists. Thus, in 1994, near Wuhan, I visited a giant new memorial site for a legendary ancient Chinese emperor.

On February 14 in ancient Rome, people would send flowers in honor of the goddess Juno. In modern times, florists and gift companies market the same day as "Valentine's Day." When selling your own products, you "accumulate money through recourse to old material" (Chen 2, p. 147). You pour "new wine into an old skein," and use venerable old names and traditions, in order to market something that is actually new. Thus, in China, various groceries are labeled as "old imperial secret recipes," or they are given names that play on old traditions.

Stratagem prevention

You must take care of your own "useless" things. You should not give them up lightly, because it is possible that they might prove useful to your competitors.

Stratagem risk

When you are "returning to life," be careful not to choose the wrong "corpse," especially if you are going to be using it in the long term.

Examples

Why bankrupt companies are so appealing

Company A, based in Hong Kong, wanted to manufacture television sets in China, but the Chinese market was already saturated. Therefore, company A was not approved by the authorities. Then, it so happened that a television factory in Guangzhou was on the verge of bankruptcy. Company A bought this "corpse," reorganized it, and rebranded the television sets that were already being made there. Thus, company A successfully entered the Chinese television market. According to Chinese stratagem authors, some Westerners also like to buy bankrupt businesses at low prices, cleverly reorganize them, and so make profits out of them (Chen 2, p. 148). Meanwhile, some architects buy houses with structural defects at very low prices, renovate them—thus injecting the "corpse" with new life—and sell them for large sums of money.

From mother's milk to her breasts

Once a product has been conceived and developed, it goes through four distinct phases: entering the market, gradually increasing its market share, reaching its sales peak, and then slowly declining. Once it is in its fourth phase, it is destined to go under completely. Unless, that is, its "corpse" can be revived. In this case, it can return to its first phase and go through all the other phases again. You can achieve this by taking an existing product and selling it as a different one. This may require subtle alterations to the original design, and often involves relaunching the product.

This is how a Taiwanese company saved a pill that promised young mothers more breast milk for their babies. At first, sales were outstanding. Then, living conditions improved, mothers found that they had quite enough milk without the pill, and improved education enabled more mothers to use powdered milk instead. Sales of the pill stagnated, and even threatened to dry up altogether. Thereupon the pharmaceutical company imbued its pill, which was already dead, with a new "soul." It claimed that the same pill would help women develop ample well-formed breasts. Thus, where the pill had previously appealed only to young mothers, it now enthused all the young ladies of Taiwan. Therefore, without changing the pill at all, the pharmaceutical company had rescued it from commercial failure (Lin, pp. 87–8).

Stratagem 15:

Luring the tiger down from the mountain [onto the plain]

In applying this stratagem, you lure your opponent away from his base, or separate him from his main allies. *Isolation stratagem.*

You cause your opponent to leave their home territory—which they know and trust and, hence, which favors them—and to go into foreign areas that you know well. This is either in order to defeat them in territory that favors you, or to occupy theirs. Thus, you lead your opponent onto "thin ice." Another variant of this stratagem is to lead your opponent far from their support personnel, thus making them easier to defeat. Here, the "tiger" represents any powerful adversary whom it would be dangerous to fight straightforwardly. But the "tiger" is also a slower-witted animal than the fox (Yu 1993, p. 135), which you have a chance of defeating by luring it away from its home terrain. You can lure the tiger away by a variety of means: You can tempt it with bait, instill fear, pretend to attack its territory, or simply provoke it.

Stratagem radius

According to the ancient Greek myth, sirens tempted passing sailors onto their island with their beautiful singing, where they killed them. Odysseus rendered their stratagem ineffective by blocking the ears of his men with wax and tying himself to the mast of his ship. Thus, his ship remained on a steady course. Unfortunately, in Heinrich Heine's poem "The Lorelei," the sailor is not so wise. High on a mountain on the bank of the Rhine, a beautiful young woman is combing her long golden hair and singing a wonderful song. Thus, she leads the sailor off course, and he perishes in the waves.

Chinese trade agreements with foreign partners tend to include certain clauses in their contracts. These oblige their partners to abandon the jurisdiction of their home country's legal system. Thus, they leave themselves at the mercy of Chinese law, which is both unfamiliar and unfavorable to them. For example, the Chinese may stipulate that the court of jurisdiction for a business contract concluded with a foreigner must be in China.

Sometimes, in the world of business, it is not really a matter of luring a competing "tiger" down from its "mountain," but of finding a "mountain" where there is currently no "tiger." You can lay claim to such "mountains" without first having to lure a "tiger" away from them. Polaroid cameras are a prime example of this: They successfully laid claim to an area of the market whose very existence the competition knew nothing about (Chen 2, pp. 160ff.).

Stratagem 15 can also be applied if the "tiger" has left the "mountain" without any encouragement. This was the policy of certain Japanese firms after World War II. European colonial powers withdrew from their colonies, leaving plenty of "mountains" without "tigers," which the Japanese exploited to the full. Their products were too basic to make any impact on Western markets, so they expanded their economic influence elsewhere, starting in Asia, Africa, and even the smallest Pacific islands, later moving on to Australia. In due course, they went into the markets of the northern hemisphere, where they were now much more successful (Lin, p. 93).

Stratagem prevention

Once you have occupied a territory, you should not give it up easily. You should carefully examine any temptation to leave your territory, and, if necessary, you should stubbornly resist it. Moreover, if you must leave your home terrain, do not stray too far away from it, and make sure that there is a way back to it. Avoid any area where you really do not feel at home. Stratagem 27, "Feigning madness without losing the balance," is an effective way to counteract stratagem 15. Thus, Wolfgang Schüssel, the Austrian chancellor, infuriates anyone who tries to lure him into their domain and make him look stupid. He is exaggeratedly laid-back, and simply will not play along with them. Instead, he devotes himself to soccer and the cello (*NZZ*, January 28, 2001, p. 3).

Stratagem risk

If you catch a shark and leave it on dry land, you render it harmless. If, however, you lure a crocodile onto the riverbank, it is still dangerous. You must make sure that you are really luring a "tiger" down onto the plain, and not an eagle. You must also make sure that your opponent really is weaker in unfamiliar territory.

Example

Using industrial strife to get rid of a manager

In 1882, Andrew Carnegie (1835–1919), the American steel magnate, bought up blocks of Henry C. Frick's stock. The latter, a former coke producer, became the deputy CEO of a jointly owned business, second in seniority only to Carnegie himself, and manager of the whole firm. It was Frick who unified all the various production centers into a single cohesive business. Thus, he created the firm that would become the largest steel company in the world (*CM*, pp. 1239–40). Nevertheless, Frick was not a pleasant man to work with, and, as the Chinese stratagem texts have it, Carnegie wanted to get rid of him. To reduce production costs and increase profits further, Frick reduced piecework pay. It did not take long for this to antagonize many people, and the unions affected by the pay cuts decided to go on strike in the Homestead factory. Behind the scenes, Carnegie gave Frick the green light to take harsh measures against the workers in this industrial dispute.[34] Here, he applied laissez-faire stratagem 16. Frick duly aggravated the situation, employing 300 strikebreakers, accompanied by armed security forces. They traveled in ships down the Monongahela River to carry out their task, and violent clashes with the strikers ensued. As a result of this intervention, 10 died and 60 were injured, and Homestead was placed under martial law (*CM*, p. 1240). Frick's reputation was ruined by this incident, and there was a failed attempt on his life shortly afterwards. All these events wore him down, and he resigned from his post. Now, Carnegie was in sole charge of the company.

A Chinese commentator describes Carnegie's conduct as an application of stratagem 15. For he succeeded in luring his "tiger," Frick, away from his "mountain," that is, his position of power in Carnegie's steel concern (Yao, p. 125).

Stratagem 16:

If one wishes to catch something, one has first to let it go

In certain situations, where you have your opponent surrounded and under pressure from all sides, there is the danger that they will use all their reserves of strength and put up fierce resistance. On such occasions, if you give your opponent a way out, they may drop their guard and be easier to deal with. "Letting them go" is not an end in itself, but it can help towards your long-term goal of "catching" them. You give something up, in order to pocket something in the future. This stratagem requires farsightedness. You must think strategically and be patient. It may take time to carry out this stratagem, but, in the end, it will not only bring you success, but will also save your energy.

Laissez-faire stratagem.

Stratagem radius

During the *cold war* (1945–1989), the Soviet Union repeatedly put the West on the defensive. The Western powers did not always have the initiative. This was an inferior position but only partially a show of weakness. For it was the restraint of the West that prevented the Kremlin's provocations from having significantly worse consequences for the world. Moreover, although they seemed unduly restrained and ready to appease the Soviets, their policy of moderation ultimately had its desired effect. Thus, the Western powers allowed the building of the Berlin Wall, taking no violent measures against it. The inaction of the West was very much in the spirit of stratagem 16, since "the construction of the wall was really an admission of defeat for communism" (*NZZ*, August 11/12, 2001, p. 7).

If your opponent is far too strong to take on directly, you can place them high on a pedestal and praise them in such exaggerated terms that they eventually become an object of ridicule, lose their authority, and cannot stay in power. This was said to have been the intention of those who took the cult of Mao Zedong to ludicrous extremes during the Cultural Revolution (1966–1976). As they say in Chinese stratagem literature, to burst a balloon, you must first inflate it as far as it will go (Yu 1993, p. 143).

A restaurant in Pittsburgh is supposed to have used a menu that did not list any prices. There was only a message to the effect that the restaurant staff trusted their diners to treat them fairly, and a request to diners to pay only as much as they saw fit. Admittedly, some customers paid too little or even nothing, but most of them actually paid more than the food was worth. On this subject, a Chinese commentator writes that most people want to appear better than they are. They want to seem generous to others, or maybe just to themselves. Consequently, the restaurant without a price list on its menu made substantial profits (Yu 1994, pp. 135–6).

Instead of launching into a big sales pitch as soon as a customer enters your store, it is much better to let your wares speak for themselves. If you leave your customers in peace, they will see what you have on offer and think about buying something. Eventually, they may even be so impressed by your wares that they start to praise them spontaneously. Hence, the best kind of advertising is subtle: If advertisements are too obtrusive, they arouse consumers' hostility (Chen 2, pp. 173–4).

Customers in places like the famous Silk Street (*Xiushuijie*) in Beijing, where until the end of 2004 there were lots of fake but useful goods on sale, were usually confronted with a trader who refused to lower his price. But if the customer applied stratagem 16, turned their back on the trader and walked away, the trader used to run after them offering a lower price.

When it comes to personnel management, or just normal human interaction, stratagem 16 can give people greater freedom, allowing their creativity to flourish, and winning their hearts by trusting in them and giving them greater autonomy. After all, "putting trust in people is a great way to awaken their hidden potential" (*QXS*, no. 2, 2004, p. 21).

Whether negotiating or just having a conversation, if you want to get the other person to speak, then it is best to stay silent. In order to break the silence, your opposite number will start speaking, and they may either make their intentions clearer, or even show signs of weakness that you can exploit. Silence also gives you time for reflection, and, in order to encourage your opponent to be self-critical, you can convey disapproval by staying quiet (Zhou 1992, pp. 46–7).

Stratagem prevention

If you think that your opponent is allowing you room to maneuver, so that you make mistakes that they can exploit, you must be extremely careful not to make such mistakes. If possible and not too risky, you should even turn the tables on them and take the opportunity to distinguish yourself and make a fool of them, or maybe just to prepare countermeasures against them. If you think that your opponent is using stratagem 16 by pretending that they do not want to do a deal with you, then you can afford to ignore their stratagem. Sooner or later, they will be knocking on your door again, and you will have the upper hand. You let a pig live, feed it well so that its meat will be of a high quality, in order to slaughter it in the end. If you establish that your opponent is treating you according to this model, then you should apply stratagem 36, "[When the situation is growing hopeless,] running away [in good time] is the best stratagem."

Stratagem risk

If you let your opponent run away at the wrong time, then "the tiger will return to its mountain" and recover its strength. If you apply stratagem 16, you have no prospect of success unless such a retreat is impossible.

Example

Burglarproof doors put to the test

Li Xiaoyun, a Chinese salesperson in the town of Loudi, in the province of Hunan, began selling Wangli burglarproof doors in 1999. Although she had tested these doors very thoroughly and found them to be of excellent quality, sadly, sales were not as good as she had expected. In fact, the citizens of Loudi didn't want to know. So Mrs. Li did some market research to find out what was wrong. It transpired that people were buying iron double doors, and having them installed in front of their existing doors. The iron doors cost only Rmb300 each, but they were not really burglarproof. Her doors were, but cost Rmb1,000 each. Then Mrs. Li took a courageous step.

She gave her doors to anyone who was interested for a "free trial" period. If the customer was satisfied, then they had to pay her for the door. But if the door did not live up to the customer's expectations, they could return the door and would not have to pay her anything. In no time, she was giving out dozens of doors. Sure enough, all the customers who tried her doors were enthusiastic about them. They liked the doors' appearance, and found them effective, convenient, and easy to use. Thus, the market grew for Wangli's excellent burglarproof doors, and, within a year, Mrs. Li was firmly established in the Loudi specialist market (*FS*, no. 10, 2003, p. 42).

Stratagem 17:
Tossing out a brick to attract jade

The "brick" symbolizes something insignificant, the "jade" something valuable. A small gift is given to someone in order to attract a large gift in return. A healthy profit is made on the back of a trifling favor. *Bait stratagem.*

Customers are attracted by good deals; a bonus can encourage staff to go the extra mile. When it comes to human interaction, a "brick" can be a friendly smile, a kind gesture, a small invitation, an encouraging word, a nice compliment, and so on. "Think about a small personal token: a little note, a book, nothing expensive—it works miracles" (*B*, November 26, 2001, p. 14).

Stratagem radius

Tax concessions and various types of preferential treatment are used in China to steer investment into quite specific areas. Many *politicians* will promise to build a bridge where there isn't even a river, just to pick up valuable votes.

According to the "Rockefeller principle," the oil magnate John D. Rockefeller (1839–1937) became rich because he introduced cheap oil lamps to people in the mid-nineteenth century, giving them away in some cases. People needed oil to light the lamps, and they got this from Rockefeller, too—but only at an inflated price.[35] Bill Gates (born 1955) occasionally gives away his software, for example, to schools (*NZZ*, October 10, 1997, p. 13), safe in the knowledge that this will bring in healthy profits later.

"The bosses of *Enron*, *WorldCom*, and other companies were so convincing in the tales of fabulous anticipated returns and increased profit that they spun to investors and banks that they all believed them" (*BZ*, July 20/21, 2002, p. 2). Credulity is the twin sister of blindness to cunning! The "fabulous anticipated returns and increased profit" were created by the bosses with the aid of creator stratagem 7, "Create something out of nothing," so that these castles in the air could be used as bricks.

To begin with, *tricksters* settle "high restaurant or hotel bills that emerge during preliminary discussions." Or they promise "invitations to special entertainment" (*Welt am Sonntag*, May 26, 2002, p. 12).

The music giant *Dieter Bohlen* was fobbed off with a senile, unusable horse as a riding mount. He bought it simply because "it was pretty cheap—DM500 below the slaughter price" (*B*, September 29, 2003, p. 8).

Stratagem prevention

The important thing in personal relationships (*guanxi*) with the Chinese is general reciprocity, even if this does not necessarily mean an immediate exchange of service and consideration. A fairly prolonged period can elapse in between. If the Chinese use stratagem 17, they will speculate on a higher consideration relative to the service itself. To prevent this, any excuse can be used to refuse a gift, or incapacitation stratagem 19 can be used, and, by way of an immediate reciprocal (that is, equivalent) return gift, any basis for the Chinese speculation of "jade" can be removed. Small tokens of goodwill should therefore be repaid one after the other with similar small tokens of goodwill. It is important to avoid any accumulation of "indebtedness," otherwise it is far too easy to become dependent. Be suspicious of generosity from people you do not know.

In addition, do not forget the Chinese saying that people who pay lip service are rarely trustworthy.

Stratagem risk

Anyone who lures people with empty promises must expect to be discovered sooner or later.

Examples

Trip to Paris

A manager with the Bull Group in France wanted to sell a chip-card system to the Shanghai Pudong Development Bank. He knew that this would involve tough negotiations, and so arranged a trip to Paris for his Chinese negotiating partner, linked to a demonstration of the technological finesse of the chip-card system concerned. This "brick" worked. Millions of Bull chip cards were subsequently used in Shanghai (*HBR*, October 2003, p. 91).

Thank-you letter for using a filling station

A filling-station owner who was new to the business was finding it hard to get ahead. Then he came up with the idea of using his customers' credit cards and car registrations to find out their addresses. From then on, he sent everyone who bought fuel at his filling station a personal thank-you letter. The result was astounding. His customers all said that they had never received a thank-you letter from a business before. The businessman's fine reputation spread in no time. People came from far and wide to fill up on his premises, putting an end to his business worries (Zhang, pp. 46–7).

Stratagem 18:
Catching the bandits by first catching the ringleader

Leader-capture stratagem; headbutt stratagem; switch-position stratagem.

The most important thing, to begin with, is to identify and "catch" the key person within the group. The objective here may be to neutralize this individual and therefore the entire group, which has thereby been deprived of its figurehead, or to win over onto your own side the individual and with them the group as a whole. In the first case, a carrot-and-stick approach can be taken; in the second, a "catch" can only be achieved using the carrot approach. Furthermore, when organizing an approach, handling an affair, or managing a company, it is important to identify and tackle the focal point, the "core business," the area of strategic importance. First identify the essential element, then put it right!

Stratagem radius

When the Queen's son, the Prince of Wales, attended the 1970 Expo in Osaka, he was met by one of the two Sony bosses, Akio Morita (1921–1999). Prince Charles asked Morita whether Sony had any plans to build a factory in Europe, and added that he hoped if Sony were to do so it would "consider Wales." In actual fact, Sony later opened a color-television factory in the Welsh town of Bridgend, which went into production in 1974. Morita naturally used his royal connection and invited Prince Charles to the factory opening as guest of honor. A commemorative plaque in English and Welsh was unveiled in his presence, thereby establishing the link between this factory and Prince Charles for time immemorial. During the early eighties, the factory was extended, and Morita once again invited Prince Charles to attend the opening. On this occasion, however, he was not available and sent instead the pregnant Diana, Princess of Wales. Morita arranged a factory tour for the princess, during which she wore a face mask and a cap bearing the Sony name. Photographs of Diana's visit to Sony's Bridgend factory were circulated throughout the English-speaking world. Diana's visit was also immortalized on a commemorative plaque. According to a Chinese book on stratagems (Yu 1994, pp. 149–50), this was a masterly use by Japan of stratagem 18.

While the first encounter with Prince Charles, which led to the skillful application of stratagem 18, was more or less handed to Akio Morita on a plate, the Beijing hotel "Long Wall" had to create the conditions in which to use the same stratagem. The hotel's general manager knew about the planned visit of the American president, Ronald Reagan, in spring 1984. Ahead of time, he set about inviting an endless stream of officials from all levels within the American embassy in Beijing to eat at his hotel, and asked them for their opinion of the service, which he then tirelessly improved. When the American embassy guests finally ran out of criticisms, the general manager went to the American embassy in Beijing with the proposal that his hotel should be awarded the contract for President Reagan's farewell banquet. After lengthy negotiations, he won the contract. On April 28, 1984, some 500 journalists from all over the world reported on this banquet, each being obliged to mention the name of the hotel, the "Long Wall"—it was an extremely effective PR exercise for the hotel, and came free of charge (Yu 1994, pp. 153–4).

Stratagem prevention

If necessary, a group leader can be rescued using stratagem 11, "Letting the plum tree wither in place of the peach tree." In any scenario, there must always be a successor ready. Above all, a leading personality must also be armed against the "carrot" approach, for example, corruption stratagem 31, if it is taken against him. Insofar as the protection of an object is concerned, spares must always be available, so that even if an opponent suddenly damages a core element, the object is guaranteed to carry on working. Total protection is never possible, but the main danger points can be covered—take an ice-hockey player with a head guard, for instance, or a soccer player with knee guards.

Stratagem risk

Take on the wrong leader and you will miss your target.

Examples

Six functions of a manager

The story goes that one day a doctor turned up in an American company, offering the manager a secret prescription. The manager was indignant, and said he would be better off caring for his patients. "Making up prescriptions for sick companies is one of my functions, too," replied the doctor, and asked him for just 20 seconds of his time. The manager allowed him the 20 seconds. The doctor said the following: "List in order of importance six activities that you, as manager, must necessarily perform in person, and carry out these functions conscientiously. Delegate all remaining activities to your staff." "And that's your prescription?" asked the manager. The doctor replied, "Try it. If you find it's useless, then you owe me nothing. But if it is effective you must pay me whatever you feel it is worth." The manager changed his working practices, based on the prescription, and achieved astonishing results. A year and a day later, the doctor received a letter with a check to the value of $25,000. According to a Chinese author, the prescription is essentially based on the fact that, in every process, the elements that are really important only constitute a relatively small percentage of all components. All that is needed is for these few essential elements to be handled correctly, for all other aspects to run relatively smoothly. So the main thing is to get hold of the "gang leader," in other words, the core functions when carrying something out (Yu 1993, p. 179).

When it comes to tackling the essential elements, the low-price German supermarket chain ALDI is king—no overbearing administration with staff offices, no unnecessary advertising, no legal department, no accounts department, no internal store finish created by an interior decorator, no press department, but instead concentration on a limited, easily visible range of goods of acceptable quality at the very lowest prices (*NZZ am Sonntag*, April 25, 2004, p. 49).

Lead a bull on a nose ring

In China, the method of defining and solving a so-called main contradiction is given as an example of the strategic application of stratagem 18 (Yu 1993, pp. 169–70; Yan, p. 68). A "main contradiction" is a central term in the official Marxist doctrine of the Chinese Communist Party. The starting point is the view that the whole world is a web of contradictions. Politics is the analysis and solution of contradictions. At each stage in its development, China's political leadership must single out one of the many coexisting contradictions, and proclaim it to be the "main contradiction." Its solution is the "main task" of the Chinese population. The entire strength of these millions of people is concentrated on this.

The Chinese Communist Party has defined the main contradiction on four occasions since 1937. From 1937 to 1945, the main contradiction was "China versus Japan." Mao Zedong allied himself to solving this main contradiction with his sworn enemy in ideological terms, Chiang Kai-shek. The main task was to defeat Japan. From 1946 to 1949, the main contradiction was the "Chinese Communist Party under Mao Zedong versus China's national government under Chiang Kai-shek." The main task was to defeat Chiang Kai-shek. From 1949 to 1976 (or rather 1978), the main contradiction was the "proletariat versus the bourgeoisie." The main task was the "class struggle." While in China, I experienced in person the last year of this phase, and the first year of the transition to the new main-contradiction phase, which has ultimately lasted since 1978. This was why I was able to study the transformation of a main contradiction at first hand. The main contradiction has remained unchanged since the end of 1978. It is "the contradiction between the growing material and cultural needs of the people and the underdeveloped social production" (Chinese Communist Party constitution, November 14, 2002, General program, section 7). This main contradiction produces the main task of the Chinese people, as the main focus around which all work (including that in foreign-trade law) must revolve—the "construction of a socialist economy." Western observers have been astounded by the huge changes that have taken place in China since 1978. But very few of them know that the driving force within the Chinese economy has its roots mainly in Chinese Marxism and in its main-contradiction method, which is reminiscent of stratagem 18.[36] In China, with its inclination towards a proletarian means of expression, easily understood by everyone, this use of stratagem 18 is rephrased with expressions like "Use the line of the fishing net to move its mesh" and "If you lead a bull, lead it by its nose ring" (Yu 2003, pp. 86ff.).

Stratagem 19:

Removing the firewood from under the cauldron

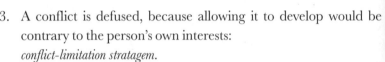

The firewood is the source of energy that causes the water in the cauldron to boil. The water cools down as soon as the firewood is removed.

The stratagem can be explained as follows.

1. A thing is tackled from the bottom up:
    root-removal stratagem.

2. The wind is taken out of someone's sails, their position is undermined, the ground is cut from under someone's feet:
    enfeeblement stratagem.

3. A conflict is defused, because allowing it to develop would be contrary to the person's own interests:
    conflict-limitation stratagem.

By applying this stratagem, you avoid meeting an opponent head-on, but instead sap their material or spiritual strength. There are many ways of incapacitating opponents. These include holding them up to ridicule. Humor undoubtedly helps to calm many tense situations. Sometimes, the aim of stratagem 19 is to destroy conditions that are favorable to an opponent.

Stratagem radius

Henry Ford (1863–1947) founded the Ford Motor Company with his financiers in 1903. It is said that a dispute with colleagues concerning the company's strategic direction almost dealt it a death blow. "Ford prevented this through an act of cunning," wrote Reiner Flick in *Die Zeit* (May 22, 2003, p. 24), although obviously without identifying the cunning technique Ford used. Instead, Flick simply recounted the events: "In 1905, he and a group of like-minded companions founded a component-manufacturing subsidiary that charged such high prices to the parent company that the entire profit remained with the subsidiary. The opposition swallowed its pride and sold its stock to Ford, as a result of which he owned 51% of the authorized capital. In 1919, he acquired the remaining stock."

In *political or other disputes*, any little thing, a minor error of detail, in what the opponent says is seized on and played on, so that the really important message loses its impact (Yu 1994, p. 54).

In 1887, the British parliament decided that German goods sold in Britain should bear the wording "Made in Germany." This was done in the belief that nobody would want to buy goods labeled "Made in Germany." As history has shown, this use of stratagem 19 proved to be foolish. Firewood was not so much removed from under the cauldron as added to it. The label "Made in Germany" gave German goods an even greater prestige, and promoted their sales worldwide.

Stratagem prevention

You must put in place double and triple protection to guard the sources of your own material and spiritual strength against possible outside enemy action. Your main resources should not be wantonly supplied to others. This is the only way of avoiding being swallowed up and losing your own mainstay. You must carefully consider all conceivable scenarios in relation to enemy action, and take the appropriate preventive measures. This is vitally important, particularly in the computer age.

Stratagem risk

If you carelessly remove firewood from under the cauldron while it is still burning, you can burn yourself. You must also be careful that the wood taken from under another's cauldron does not turn out to be the branch you're sitting on.

Examples

A recipe for success from America

From a Chinese standpoint, America uses stratagem 19 formidably and highly successfully in strategic terms (Zhang, pp. 213–14). After World War II, many of Germany's top scientists were transferred to America; these included Wernher von Braun, who was the driving force behind the first moon landing. For decades, America has succeeded in attracting the most highly qualified people from all over the world through a variety of incentives (stratagem 17), and has allowed them into its country. The two main attractions are probably high salaries and outstanding research conditions. Frustrated with German bureaucracy in higher education, one in seven scientists flees to America and some 400,000 top professionals from the European Union work in America (*RRH*, December 29, 2003, p. 11). By attracting the best professionals from other countries where they were trained and educated, America also saves on its own education and training costs. It not only removes the firewood from under the other's cauldron, but repeatedly places the new firewood under its own cauldron, too. "Because America gets on so well by attracting the world's elite scientists and getting them to work for it, the country has succeeded in forging ahead to become the world's leader in scientific development. The scientific development promoted an economic boom, leading to America becoming the richest nation on earth" (Lin, p. 141). What in China is interpreted in terms of stratagem 19 is described as follows in German-language announcements: "For decades, the Americans have made huge efforts to attract the world's best university teachers to their country. After China, India, Taiwan, and Britain, Germany is one of the most important countries concerned. As German scientists leave, the German minister of education, Edelgard Bulmahn, claims they are subsidizing American research" (*Der Spiegel*, no. 4, 2001, p. 144). However, it could also occur to you to say that the use of stratagem

19 is not alien to China when it comes to the planning of its foreign-trade activities; indeed, many German companies and German nationals are increasingly getting the uneasy feeling that "they will soon be bled dry by the powerful partner and robbed of their technological lead" (*FAZ*, December 5, 2003, p. 1). Such analyses, which identify the West overall as the potential victim of the stratagem, are also fueled by the displacement of parts of industrial production and the wholesale movement of assets to Asia.

Disarmament through self-criticism

Applying this stratagem involves following the maxim "If you don't want anyone to know what you've done, it is better not to have done it in the first place" (*Ruo yao ren bu zhi, chu fei ji mo wei*). In this way, you escape reproaches and criticism on the safest foundation. If you are caught out on some impropriety, immediately disclosing the whole picture will do more to disarm the opponent and defuse the situation than any frantic attempt to deny the incident. "Bravely confess your own omission or error. No one is without failing. Rather than thinking little of them or even treating them with contempt, the Chinese regard those who openly accept their inadequacies and shortcomings as the intelligent ones. On the other hand, the know-it-alls who claim to do everything right are despised by their colleagues."[37] This advice, which is redolent of the spirit of stratagem 19 and, also to some extent, that of stratagem 34, is something I can only pass on from my experience of living in Beijing (1975–1977). A Western colleague, a China consultant well versed in the 36 stratagems, even told me that in critical situations he would kneel theatrically before Chinese managers or official representatives and apologize verbosely—with optimal effect each time.

Stratagem 20:

Clouding the water to catch the fish [robbed of their clear sight]

Stratagem of stirring things up, or of exploiting obscurity/disorder/confusion.

Murkiness stratagem; confusion stratagem; chaos stratagem.

The basis and starting point for this stratagem is the unclearness, ambiguity, and complexity of the world in general and the marketplace in particular. The world is essentially "cloudy" or "murky." Consequently, there is plenty of opportunity to fish in murky waters. If the world or the thinking of individuals should, exceptionally and for once, be clear, then this stratagem will result in them both being obscured, for example, with the help of provocation stratagem 13, and advantages will be gained from the artificially created obscurity.

Stratagem radius

In China, many producers "cloud the water" by choosing a brand name for their product that is easily confused with a famous brand name, for example, "Hongda," which is suggestive of the Japanese brand "Honda" (Yu 2003, p. 100).

Stratagem 20 is used by authorities that squander taxpayers' money, protected by the lack of transparency in government administration; see the *Schwarzbuch der öffentlichen Verschwendung (Black Book of Public Waste)* published by the German Taxpayers' Federation. "The state has debts of €1.3 billion—€16 per head of the population. Money is squandered on bridges without roads leading to them, unnecessary computers, the finest granite for provincial railroad stations. According to the Taxpayers' Federation, €30 billion are frittered away every year" (*B*, April 5, 2004, p. 9).

Projects are inflated unnecessarily or even executed without anybody needing them. As a result, there are no funds left in the budget for urgent items such as schools, hospitals, or police computers.

Lack of transparency is exploited in large complex groups: Executives, even going as high as CEOs, try to get an advantage over their supervisory bodies, which no longer have a complete overview.

Stratagem 20 is also used liguistically: customers are taken in by unclear wording. A large electrical-appliance business in the Inner Mongolia Autonomous Region announced that on a given day color televisions would be sold for only Rmb500 instead of Rmb1,000. When the store opened early that morning, there were already nearly 100 customers waiting, some of whom had traveled a long way. It emerged that there were only three televisions available at the low price. If the customers had read the advertising copy carefully, they would have realized that it did not specify how many color televisions were to be discounted. The advertising copy, which did not actually contain any lies, simply stated that customers would be dealt with on a first come, first served basis.

Stratagem prevention

By creating small transparent areas of responsibility, or by means of genuinely effective (but flexible and nonrepressive) control measures, stratagem 20 can be resisted. To avoid confusion—the breeding ground of stratagem 20—unclear instructions and measures must be avoided, as must poor communication, inadequate reply mechanisms, contradictory statements and signals, and the loss of reliable forms of personal support. In a chaotic situation, it is important not to overreact, because this only generates more confusion.

Statements made by an opposite number should be closely checked for intelligibility. If you yourself have a clear plan, you must represent it unequivocally without allowing fuzzy wording to creep in, otherwise you will leave the way open for your opponent to use stratagem 20.

To deflect the stratagem in a negotiating context, the very first thing to do is focus clearly on the goal without allowing yourself to be sidetracked. Insofar as there is any lack of clarity, this must be cleared up first, before there is any further negotiation. If the opposing side attempts to disrupt the negotiating process, it is important to insist on the individual items being dealt with in the order anticipated. If necessary, you must have the courage to say that you do not understand what the opponent means, or even make it clear to them that the negotiations should not be prejudiced by digression.

In addition, you should always be alert to people who claim that things are clear, and do not be taken in by them. Keep a clear head in the face of sudden "murkiness," to avoid falling victim to anyone fishing in the murky waters! A nontransparent situation should be tolerated, without having an eye to gurus claiming to have insight.

The fact that nearly one in ten laws passed by the German parliament is defective, and has to be "amended" by peoples' representatives (*B*, April 5, 2004, p. 9), should provoke some thought. Legislators should think of all eventualities, rather than blindly passing a series of laws that contain more holes than a piece of Emmental cheese, and that encourage the people to fish in murky waters instead of inspiring faith in the law.

Stratagem risk

Vagueness in your own formulations, when announcing measures and so on, can allow room for maneuver, but it can be counterproductive, too. "The people would like proper reforms, but they would also like to know beforehand where the journey is leading. With the policy currently being pursued by the German government, the target direction is still unclear" (*NZZ*, April 13, 2004, p. 29).

As a stratagem user, you should avoid falling victim to the "murkiness of the water" yourself, and losing your own clear-sightedness. Also, you should go after the right and not the wrong "fish" in the "murky waters."

Examples

Always in the same breath as the big ones

Immediately after World War II, the Japanese construction market was dominated by five major construction companies of renown. The market situation was completely transparent to this extent. However, there was still a small company, whose ambitious director was determined to become one of the major companies. To achieve this, he paid substantial sums of money to the country's main newspapers and agreed that whenever an advertisement was placed for one of the five major construction companies, one would be added for his own company, too. Conversely, in advertisements for his own company, he always made sure that the other five companies were mentioned in the same breath as his own. In this way, he hoodwinked the public into overestimating the true size of his company. However, thanks to the advertisements, the number of customers grew and, rather than being disappointed with the company, they were naturally satisfied with the top-quality work. Three years later, thanks to the use of stratagem 20, by which he was able to make the public believe that there were six major construction companies, including his own, and also thanks to his company's impeccable work, the director was able to achieve his goal. His company actually became the sixth biggest construction company in Japan (Lin, pp. 198–9).

Negotiating confusion

In price negotiations, rather than putting your cards on the table right from the very beginning, you leave your opposite number in doubt as to your actual margins (Zhou 1992, p. 60). In order to confuse an opponent, a simple question can be complicated; things that actually have nothing to do with each other can be intertwined; or subjects that have already been discussed can be raised once again. If the opponent makes a demand that cannot be met, the opposite number's message can be deliberately misunderstood. To correct the assumed misunderstanding, the opponent feels obliged to give clarifications and explanations, which affects their concentration on their own concerns. Hence, company A suddenly demanded a 2.5% price reduction, after a cooperation agreement with company B had already been concluded. Company B's negotiating team retired for an hour before saying, "We have amended the list prices as required by A, but we now have to talk through the contractual services that will have to be dropped." Company A replied that there had been a misunderstanding and that company B still had to provide all the originally specified services. Company B was able to use the resulting confusion on the price-reduction issue to achieve a compromise that suited both sides (Yu 1994, pp. 164–5).

Stratagem 22:
Shutting the door to capture the thief

Enclosure stratagem; encirclement stratagem; entrapment stratagem.

The aim of this stratagem is to make it impossible for a defeated opponent to escape, by exploiting the isolated position that they have either accepted voluntarily or been enticed into. The stratagem can only succeed if the enclosure is impregnable, the closed door impenetrable, and the bolted room without opening.

Stratagem radius

Economy: A shopping center or mall in which a wide variety of stores and establishments covers all the customers' needs, so that they have no inclination to shop elsewhere, and an individual store that constantly provides a service that looks after its customers' every need (Lin, p. 126) are considered in the Chinese stratagem literature to be applications of this stratagem (Chen 2, pp. 226–7).

World politics: "'China is the only great power preparing to fight the US in a military sense,' says John Tkacick, an analyst at the Washington-based Heritage Foundation. Mr Tkacick argues that the Chinese are not necessarily America's enemies but should not be portrayed as 'our friends.' 'If you look at the US strategic presence in Asia,' says Mr Gershman, 'their position is better than anything they could have imagined. If China is the enemy of the future, then the US has got a lot of what it wanted, without saying that China is the enemy.' Not that the war on terrorism is considered by the administration as a discreet ruse to reapportion resources without triggering Beijing's ire. As Ms Rice put it this week, Iraq may be the 'central front' in the war on terror, but Asia is a 'very important front'." (*Financial Times*, October 17, 2003, p. 13). Those Chinese who are well versed in stratagems can interpret these somewhat guarded analyses only from the standpoint of stratagem 22. Put simply, as far as they are concerned, the lines quoted mean that America has erected a network of military bases around China, and particularly in the Commonwealth of Independent States bordering China, in anticipation of a future "high noon" with the country, with the intention of fencing it in; yet, so that this does not appear to be the case, the network has been created under the cloak of the "war against terror."

Rhetoric: Skillful questioning can drive a dialogue partner into a corner. In negotiations, it may be advisable to nail down the opposite number to a position.

Stratagem prevention

You should never put your head "in the tiger's mouth." According to the third of the ten secret rules of the board-game, Go, you should "enter another area cautiously" and always ensure you have a secure way out. The ground onto which you are moving, possibly with the aid of information stratagems, for example, stratagem 13, "Beating the grass to startle the snakes," should be tested for danger.

Stratagem risk

Regulation fury and control hysteria can turn stratagem 22 into a foolish act, by which you virtually lock yourself in a room, putting yourself out of action. Likewise, in foolish actions directed against themselves, managers transform stratagem 22 when they protect themselves with consultants and advisers, go into retreat, and "live in a world of illusion." If, in commercial and other disputes, the captured "thief" is inadvertently pushed to extremes, there is a danger that "the hunted dog will jump over the wall" or "the cat forced into a corner will turn into a tiger."

Examples

His own customer

Despite all warnings, the Taiwanese industrialist Wang Yongqing set up the first plastics-manufacturing factory in Taiwan in the fifties. Each month, he produced 100 (metric) tons, but was only able to sell 20. He then reduced his production costs and retail prices, in order to tap into new markets abroad, too. But due to the transportation costs and far cheaper Japanese plastic, Wang Yongqing was unable to bring things into line. He sat on his goods like a thief locked in a room. Yet, he managed to free himself from the dead-end street he had gone down. He opened a new factory, this time to produce plastic products, and proceeded to sell the raw plastic to himself.

From that point on, the business operated with both factories. Wang Yongqing's business emporium grew and grew, and now employs over 40,000 staff (Zhang, pp. 249ff.).

Start of negotiations a week before Christmas

The Chinese announced to a Western delegation a deadline for the end of negotiations and a preorganized contract-signing ceremony that was to take place then. This forced the Western delegation into a time frame. Either that or the Western delegation would be invited to contract negotiations in China commencing December 17, in other words, a week before Christmas.

According to another variant of the stratagem's application, the Western delegation was sworn into a particular "spirit" in which the contract was to be held and particular "principles," for example, in the form of a declaration of intent, after which it was put under pressure to accept certain specific clauses, this being the only way of fulfilling the agreed "spirit" of the contract and the agreed "principles."

Standard or draft contracts prepared by the Chinese, which foreign firms are forced to accept and from which a "breakout" is barely possible, are related to stratagem 22 (Fang, p. 270).

Stratagem 23:
Befriending a distant enemy to attack an enemy nearby

Stratagem of temporary distant friendship/alliance; hegemony stratagem.

In the usual political sense, this stratagem may be applied when faced with several strategic opponents, and is based on their tactical weighting according to the "nearness" and "distance" criterion. A nearby strategic opponent is isolated by a tactical alliance with a distant strategic rival, in order to eliminate the nearby rival followed by the distant one. "Nearby" and "distant" should not simply be viewed in geographical terms, but also in the context of a strategic opponent who is particularly troublesome, or, in other words, "nearby," and another strategic opponent whose pressure is felt slightly less, and is therefore "distant."

In the economic sector, the literal meaning of the formula of stratagem 23 tends to be observed: "Join forces at a distance to attack nearby." According to this less military-sounding wording, which is open to numerous interpretations, the stratagem is related, for example, to a foreign company with advanced technology and to a Chinese company that seeks to profit from this technology. The Chinese company agrees to join forces with the foreign company, say, to form a joint venture, in order to get its hands on the foreign technology. This is the "distant alliance." Its purpose is a "nearby attack," in other words, the increase in competitiveness of the Chinese company on the domestic market. A more far-reaching goal, though, involves a "distant attack" later, too, in other words, conquering foreign markets. The Chinese speak of Japan's success in using this system during the sixties (Yu 1994, pp. 190–1).

Stratagem radius

Chinese foreign policy: A few years before his death in 1976, Mao Zedong developed his theory of three worlds. The "first world" included the two superpowers, America and the Soviet Union. The "second world" consisted of the nations of Europe, who were within the American and Russian sphere of influence, as well as Canada, Australia, and Japan. The "third world" comprised the nations of Asia, Africa, and Latin America, who were formally colonized by the European forces. China belonged to the "third world." For Mao, the "main contradiction" on a global scale was the contradiction between the third and the first world. In other words, China regarded America and the Soviet Union as its main enemies. Of the two nations making up the first world—America and the Soviet Union—the latter had a direct border with China, and therefore appeared particularly dangerous. This analysis led Mao to conclude that, in the spirit of stratagem 23, China must ally itself to the distant enemy, so as to be able to hold in check the nearby enemy, in other words, the Soviet Union. This is what led to Nixon's visit to China in 1972, right in the middle of the Cultural Revolution (1966–1976), and ultimately to the creation of diplomatic relations between China and America in 1979.

Construction of the Chinese economy: The socialist modernization program that began in 1978 is not unaffected by stratagem 23 either. Under this program, set in motion by the third plenary session of the eleventh central committee of the Chinese Communist Party in December 1978, China has experienced the longest phase of uninterrupted, peaceful construction since the first Opium War (1839–1842). During this phase, which is set to last well into the twenty-first century, the main contradiction, in a nutshell, is "the need for modernization versus underdevelopment" (see also stratagem 18). In order to overcome this most important and disturbing contradiction, China is once again reliant on the goodwill of distant rivals like America and European nations. Only with their technical and financial help will it be possible to do away with the most obvious current enemy, namely, poverty and underdevelopment at home.

Stratagem prevention

Under no circumstances should an alliance with a distant opponent, which can be entered into with the appropriate care and protection of one's own interests, be regarded as a steadfast reassurance. You must always be on your guard with the allied distant opponent— otherwise you may get a rude awakening. You must guard against your own possible isolation by maintaining widespread contacts.

Stratagem risk

Distant water will not extinguish a nearby fire. Above all, stratagem 23 is no panacea if the country using it is small and weak. In an emergency, it risks being allowed to go under by its distant allies.

Example

Li Ka-Shing in a triangular relationship

Kowloon Dock, the biggest dock in Hong Kong, was worth HK$1.8 billion. There was no doubt that the dock was tremendously important to the ship-owning magnate Pao Yue-kong (1918–1991). Procuring this dock would have meant he owned the major part of Hong Kong's packing and transportation industry. However, the dock was not yet his; it was still in the hands of the group Jardine Matheson & Co. The tycoon Li Ka-Shing (born 1928) had also cast a longing glance at Kowloon Dock. However, he also had plans to appropriate the conglomerate Hutchison-Whampoa Ltd. Li Ka-Shing could not pursue both goals with the same vigor. As a result, he concentrated on the acquisition of Hutchison-Whampoa, only devoting half his energies to the Kowloon Dock project.

Pao Yue-kong analyzed his two opponents, and the trilateral relationship between them and himself. If all three fought against each other individually, none of them would carry off a victory. But if two parties, it didn't matter which, formed an allegiance, the third party would have to climb down. Which party should he opt for? He decided on Li Ka-Shing. Because he did not give Kowloon Dock absolute priority, he was a "distant enemy." By contrast, Jardine Matheson didn't want to give an inch of its hold over the dock, making it the most troublesome opponent, and therefore the "nearby enemy." Consequently, he had to join forces with Li Ka-Shing against Jardine Matheson.

Pao Yue-kong spontaneously sold Li Ka-Shing 90 million stocks in the Hutchison-Whampoa group, thereby helping him gain more influence in the battle for this group. In return, he received 20 million stocks in Kowloon Dock from Li Ka-Shing. He later beat Jardine Matheson to it, and managed to get a further 20 million stocks in the dock, finally making him the majority stockholder in the much sought-after dock.

All three parties were rivals in relation to Kowloon Dock, but at different levels. Pao Yue-kong came out on top, because he made an allegiance with the "distant" party, with whom there was only a relatively weak conflict of interest, and the main direction of impact was against the "nearby" party, whose interests clashed directly with his own.

Stratagem 28:
Removing the ladder after [the opponent] has climbed onto the roof

Blind-alley stratagem; neutralizing stratagem; exit-thwarting stratagem.

Someone is guided into a position from which there is no going back or that takes them out of play.

Stratagem radius

Guidance method: You maneuver yourself (or someone else) into a position where your (or their) back is to the wall, in order to spur yourself (or others) on to the highest achievements. General de Gaulle, for instance, always went all out, leaving himself no room for retreat. As the president of France, he made every referendum a vote for him or against him.

Customer capture: Ways and means can be found to make a customer stay put, for example, through customer cards, loyalty awards, bonus programs, or threatening the customer with financial losses if they switch from company A to company B.

Auctions: The seller's staff mingle among the customers incognito to drive up the price, before bailing out just before a customer places their last (and excessively high) bid (Yu 1994, p. 227).

Holdup: An employee receives expensive training from an employer, and later uses the money invested by the employer to make unanticipated salary demands, to which the latter must accede, like it or not.

Lock-in: Special offers entice customers to make a purchase, for example, through cheap records or cheap fax machines. The snag is that the records can only be played using a particular record player, which then has to be bought separately, and the toner for the fax machine is extremely expensive. The same applies to a cheap car with expensive parts.

A loving couple in earlier times: The woman breaks it to the man that she is pregnant, so marriage is unavoidable.

A lamb to the slaughter: A person is moved to a post that is already known to be unsuitable for them, and hung out to dry with their incompetence on show for all to see.

Stratagem prevention

The prerequisites for avoiding such malevolent job offers are self-knowledge and self-moderation, as well as the struggle against excessive ambition. In relation to inventions like the atomic bomb and biotechnology, people should be sufficiently alive to cunning to recognize that they are using stratagem 28 against themselves: once such things have been invented, there's no way of going back.

Stratagem risk

If you bid too high in negotiations or career steps, you can take a painful tumble from the roof you have landed on without a ladder. In this case, you will have used the stratagem against yourself, but in a foolish way.

Examples

The impending departure

With the aid of stratagem 1, the Chinese company A had lured the German company B to China, to conduct premature contractual negotiations on a joint venture. There was scarcely enough time for the numerous differences in opinion to be ironed out. Finally, the German delegation's departure was imminent. A number of contractual points still had to be resolved in both the Chinese and the English versions of the contract, because the chairman of the Chinese company repeatedly sought amendments to the English text when it had just been finalized by both sides. There was no time left for the final English version of the contract to be translated into Chinese. Stratagem 1 ultimately proved detrimental to the Chinese side. Unless they were willing to allow the contract to fall apart at the last minute, there was nothing for it other than to acknowledge the English-language version of the contract document, which had at least been agreed, as the prevailing text.[38] Normally, Chinese contractual partners in joint ventures will endeavor to establish the Chinese-language contract documents as the only basis.

Here, the German side proved quite spontaneously to be skillful users of the blind-alley stratagem—albeit probably unaware that they had applied it. The Chinese and Germans had got onto the roof, in other words, they had agreed on the contents of the contract based on the English version. The fact that the Germans pointed to their undeferrable homeward flight forced the Chinese to reach for a most disagreeable ladder, in the form of a concession with regard to the prevailing contractual text being in the English rather than the Chinese language.

The mysterious barrel of wine

There is a report of a wine store in Bangkok where the owner placed a huge barrel of wine at the entrance, which attracted everyone's attention. As people drew closer, they saw the inscription "Unauthorized looking into this barrel prohibited." This ban attracted passers-by to take a look in the barrel—suddenly they had placed their head in the abyss. A delightful whiff of alcohol immediately accosted their senses, and, at the same time, they saw a caption written inside the barrel: "Our store sells amazing wines— just try them!" This advertisement is based on stratagem 28. First, it entices people and gets them to look inside the barrel. But, once they have looked inside, the wheel cannot be turned back. The ladder has been removed. The wine's seductive aroma has unquestionably taken hold, and knowledge of the advertising message cannot be reversed either. "Gotcha!" shout passers-by, usually laughing, and most of them, their curiosity aroused, make a return visit to the wine store (Zhang, pp. 318–19).

Stratagem 30:
Turning [the role of] the guest into [that of] the host

Stratagem of unnoticed appropriation of a position of power; infiltration stratagem; cuckoo stratagem; usurping-of-power stratagem; gaining-the-upper-hand stratagem.

The host shows the guest to a place at the dining table, arranges for the food to be served, then finally makes it clear that they can leave. In an interpersonal relationship, therefore, "guest" stands for the passive, subordinate party and "host" for the active, superior one. Stratagem 30 aims to achieve a role reversal, with the "guest" achieving the status of "host," and the latter being relegated to "guest."

Inspired by this stratagem, you can make constant inquiries during negotiations, firstly to force the opposing side onto the defensive, and secondly, to uncover possible weaknesses in their plan. Weaknesses that can be established by scrutinizing the dossier, or other dark points on the part of the opposing side that have anyway been ascertained through research, and for which the opposing party can be rebuked, can be used to reverse your own defensive, subordinate negotiating position (Yu 1994, p. 250). The upper hand can also be gained, or won back, by suddenly giving way or, conversely, by allowing the negotiations to reach deadlock. If you make the opposing side hugely aware of their need for the product you are selling, you can strengthen your own position. If you pursue a business policy in which the "customer is king," you can also consider yourself in the metaphorical sense to be a user of this stratagem (Yu 1994, p. 245). By anticipating all your customer's wishes, you give him the impression of being dominant.

Stratagem radius

In 50:50 joint ventures between China and the West, the Chinese management will sometimes take control, sooner or later, if the Western side is not careful (*HBM*, November 2003, pp. 64ff.).

The conductors on a particular bus line in a Chinese town are notorious for failing to give the correct change when tickets are purchased. One passenger solves the problem by using stratagem 30, and only hands over the Rmb10 banknote once the conductor has given the full Rmb9 back in change for the ticket.

Country A asks country B for military support, against rebels, for instance. Country B later leaves its troops in country A and determines policy there.

Financial backers, lobbyists, or other influential people look for a politician with a blemished record to sponsor. Once they have shoehorned the politician into office, the financial backers turn the politician into a compliant tool of theirs, because they can threaten at any time to rake up the politician's former misdemeanors in public, and thereby destroy them. Or a particularly dim-witted politician is made president of a country, because they can be surrounded by advisers who can enforce the policy of people in the shadows, without being seen through or obstructed by the foolish figurehead. If anything should go wrong, the president naturally takes the rap.

From time to time, when appointing staff in universities, on municipal councils, in companies, and so on, the least capable applicant in each case is deliberately appointed. This is a way of ensuring that the incumbent staff member remains in control, and is never overshadowed by the new colleague or driven by their achievements to new efforts.

Certain people in conversations love not only puffing themselves up by using words, but also expressing their authority through body language and provoking submissive signals in their opposite number. An example of this is people who fix their gaze rigidly; they are not usually accustomed to the other person holding their arrogant gaze and simply staring back (*FAZ*, February 21, 2004, p. 51).

Stratagem prevention

If you have a leading position in the marketplace, there can be no easing off. You must take every competitor seriously, however small, because they could successfully apply stratagem 30. You should determinedly follow the competition's moves, paying particular attention to their seemingly foolhardy ideas. During the sixties, American car companies with their giant limousines were too slow to notice how the Japanese car industry was flooding the American market with its more streamlined vehicles (Lin, p. 167).

In negotiations, you should staunchly maintain your position, constantly checking that your opponent has not found ways and means of achieving a dominant position. Consequently, when it comes to the location for negotiations, you should use the home advantage just as often as your Chinese partner, rather than allowing yourself to be constantly invited to the Middle Kingdom. Don't let yourself be intimidated!

From a strategic standpoint, in other words, looking slightly further into the future, the following utterances should be considered as stratagem-preventive signs. According to Frank Sieren, long-time Beijing correspondent on the German weekly economics magazine *Wirtschaftswoche*, the Middle Kingdom has "spun a fine web of globalization" around the West, including America, in which interdependences are created, and which may, in the not-too-distant future, lead to a *role change* between the economic rivals Europe and China. China has left behind the other developing countries, like Russia, India, the Asian tigers, and also Japan, which proved too small, too expensive, and too inflexible, and "is wresting the market leadership from its Western rivals, one after the other" (*NZZ*, February 3, 2004, p. 42).

Stratagem risk

Sometimes dominance can also be counterproductive, and should not therefore be strived for. Hence, the People's Republic of China, unlike America, is wary of openly articulated claims to a global, or even only a regional, "leading role."

Examples

Change of owner at McDonald's

Raymond A. Kroc (1902–1984) sold paper cups and later mixers. Already close to retirement, in 1954, at the age of 52, he went into a burger bar run by the McDonald brothers during a business trip to California. He was struck by the throng of customers. What impressed him most was the way in which the restaurant was run. The McDonald brothers operated a sort of conveyor belt on which the burgers were made. Eight mixer units could supply 40 milk shakes simultaneously. Only plastic cutlery and paper napkins were used, enabling cleaning costs to be lowered and the restaurant to be cleaned more quickly. The operation was so efficiently organized that customers were served within 60 seconds. Although the selection of products was limited, the food on offer was very reasonably priced. Ray Kroc was immediately captivated by this concept (*CM*, p. 1336), and he immediately set about applying stratagem 30 (Yu 1994, p. 246). In order to make himself the "guest," Kroc acquired from the McDonald brothers the license to run in their name, on a franchise basis, a chain of fast-food restaurants organized according to their concept. He introduced his own innovations, such as standardizing the size of the burger and accompanying the burger with a precisely defined number of onion rings. In this way, he optimized the McDonald brothers' business concept. The first branch of McDonald's opened in 1955 in Illinois. Kroc had financial difficulties to begin with. In 1960, he earned profits of only $139,000. But he strived for improvement. In the meantime, he had ingratiated himself with the McDonald brothers to such an extent that, in 1961, he persuaded them to be cut out of the company completely in return for a compensation payment of $2.7 million. The "guest" had become the "host." Kroc launched a massive advertising campaign, which was followed slowly but surely by the milestones in the development of McDonald's. In 1963 the five-hundredth restaurant was opened abroad, and in 1967 the first outlet in a foreign country. In the seventies, Kroc's fortune already amounted to $500 million.

Incidentally, thousands had already gone into the restaurant before Kroc, but none of them had recognized the potential of the McDonald brothers' fast-food concept. It was Kroc who recognized the "sheep" and "led it away" (stratagem 12).

Displacement of trademarks on the Chinese market

China's dependence on foreign countries is gradually growing through its sharp increase in imports. Yet, through a network of regulations anchored in extremely exhaustive economic legislation, the People's Republic of China ensures in accordance with a polarity norm[39]—"self-reliance as fundamental, striving after foreign assistance as secondary," and maintaining one's "economic security" (*jingji anquan*)—that the many foreign companies in China in all phases of their development are ultimately subject to Chinese control, and, for example, are never able to exert a determining influence on Chinese domestic or foreign policy. Foreign political lobbyists are unheard of in the People's Republic of China. Through high rates of local content, which are written into joint ventures, in other words, the compulsion to produce a progressively higher proportion of product parts on site in China as each year goes by, the transfer of know-how is curbed, dependence on foreign imports reduced, jobs created, and China's self-sufficiency increased. Prudently operating without Exxon Mobil and Shell, who had pushed for inclusion, PetroChina, the world's fourth largest oil group in terms of reserves, is producing the 4,000-kilometer-long gas pipeline to Shanghai (*Finanz€n*, Munich, no. 4, April 1, 2004, pp. 33–4). With its currency policy, too, the People's Republic of China guarantees that it cannot be troubled by foreign crises, in other words, it cannot be forced away from its role as "host" in the Chinese economy. Despite all these measures aimed at securing the "host" role, the Chinese complain about the successful application of stratagem 30 by foreign companies. For instance, they establish joint ventures with Chinese partners that have a famous Chinese brand name, who then become the owner of the trademark concerned. Later, the foreign partners in the joint venture ensure that the Chinese trademark is put on ice and replaced with the foreign trademark, which inherits the old trademark's customer base (Li, pp. 322ff.).

Stratagem 31:
The stratagem of the beautiful man/woman

Adonis/Venus trap; sex or decoy stratagem; corruption stratagem.

This stratagem usually relates to beautiful women. From a Chinese standpoint, in the past this stratagem was used not by beautiful women of their own volition, but rather by men who used them to achieve their goals. The women were therefore usually instruments, rather than players, in this stratagem.

The thinking whereby cunning is first and foremost a weapon of the weak, and therefore of women, is far less widespread in China than it is in the West. It may be that in the West men created this myth, in order to divert attention away from their own cunning. In examples of stratagems from present-day China, however, women are increasingly using this particular stratagem for their own ends (Fu, pp. 171–2). By using a beautiful woman, the opponent can be corrupted. Corruption through the female art of love is seen as one typical form of corruption. Consequently, any sort of corruption is classed as an application of this stratagem.

Stratagem radius

In *advertising*, this stratagem is common practice worldwide (Li, pp. 330ff.). In this case, there is an evident trend towards the woman being used as an instrument.

Sales staff in local stores are recommended to target this stratagem at "young couples." Attention should be focused on the woman, and on arousing in her the desire to purchase an even more expensive product. The man, for fear of losing face in front of his partner, will in most cases show generosity and buy the woman what she wants, even if he doesn't have much money (Yu 1994, p. 264).

Stratagem prevention

There is a Chinese saying that goes, "A fly can only get into a hen's egg if it is cracked" (Chen 2, p. 320). Anyone seeking to resist stratagem 31 must be immune to sexual and other forms of corruption, for example, through self-discipline. In any event, one should remain wary of "beautiful people" who suddenly appear, and make in-depth inquiries before getting mixed up with them.

Stratagem risk

The stratagem makes a victim of the opponent through his own weakness. Even if he later realizes what was going on with the beautiful woman, there will not usually be any great feeling of resentment. Consequently, the stratagem, insofar as it works with a physically beautiful woman, is relatively risk-free. Obviously, the stratagem user must take care that the woman does not fall in love with the victim, and switch sides. If the stratagem of the beautiful woman is used in advertising, it is important to ensure that she doesn't steal the show from the product.

If bribes and other material means are used in accordance with this stratagem to corrupt people, the offender runs the risk of being called to account under both civil and criminal law. Legal "corruption" measures taken by Chinese business partners sometimes end badly, particularly in the area of foreign trade. For instance, the Chinese side organizes an excessively lavish banquet for the foreign business partner, so that the latter, rather than being captivated by this, on the contrary feels repelled or starts to doubt the judgment of the Chinese counterpart, and gives up any plans of working with the Chinese partner concerned.

Example

Kissing competition in Tianjin

The supermarket "Everyone's Fortune" in Tianjin announced a kissing competition. It was arranged for Valentine's Day, 2004. Couples could enter from February 10, 2004, onward. The pair that kissed for the longest during the competition could expect to take away 2,000 Chinese dollars in cash. There were naturally protests. Older Chinese claimed this sort of marketing did not conform to the traditionally reserved nature of the Chinese. Younger Chinese had no quarrel with the kissing competition. One student said that the emphasis nowadays was on individuality, and kissing was just as normal as handshaking. The lively discussion helped to ensure that the supermarket's sexuality-based PR campaign fully achieved its advertising objective. Even the overseas issue of the Chinese Communist Party publication the *People's Newspaper* carried a report on it (*RRH*, February 6, 2004, p. 4).

Stratagem 33:
The special agent stratagem/The stratagem of sowing discord

1. *Subverting stratagem; agent-provocateur stratagem; destabilization stratagem;*
2. *mischief-maker stratagem.*

Originally at the forefront of this stratagem was the stirring-up of discord by a special agent fed into a group to create division. In a more general sense, the aim of this stratagem is to divide several allied opponents, by spreading rumors, targeting misinformation, exaggerating or concealing individual facts, treating different group members unequally, and so on. With regard to the economy, although the stratagem still relates to the creation and/or use of contradictions, it also frequently involves industrial espionage without activities leading to the creation of divisions.

Stratagem radius

Power politics: "Divide and conquer" was, and still is, a frequently used method of exercising and extending power. It is particularly easy to create a division between European states. One need think only of the American distinction between "old" and "new" Europe, and the undiplomatic reactions of Jacques Chirac to such American attempts at division.

Company sale: A sells to the large entrepreneur B its comparatively small, but nevertheless for B annoying, rival company on condition that B employs the experienced technician T from the purchased company. B agrees to employ T, and A founds a new company. B later entrusts the technician T with negotiating the purchase of a patent that is absolutely crucial to B's continuing prosperity. During the negotiations, T admits to the patent holder that he is A's confidential agent, and offers the patent-holder a higher price for the patent than B, as well as the post of chief engineer in A's newly formed company. The patent-holder, inexperienced in matters of business, sells his patent to A. It emerges that A only sold the company to B in order to get their agent T in place, so that he could work for them when the time was right. Because A now owns the vital patent, B must agree most reluctantly to a merger with A's company, and appoint A as general manager of the newly formed company (Zhang, pp. 98ff.).

In the guise of tourists, journalists, actors, immigrants, students, businesspeople, and so on, those involved in *industrial espionage* (Yu 1993, p. 6), constituting 70–80% of the world's total spy population (Yu 1994, p. 279), implement this stratagem.

When *negotiations* take place between foreign businesses and companies in the People's Republic of China, if there are ethnic Chinese in the foreign delegation, it is possible that the Chinese side will attempt to play them off against the non-Chinese members of the delegation concerned (Fang, p. 274).

Chinese foreign-trade policy: Based on their method of contradiction analysis, the Chinese business community uses the contradictions existing between Western states, for example, France and America, and Western companies, for example, Volkswagen and General Motors, or else they feed these contradictions and play rivals off against each other left, right, and center, in order to achieve the best possible business outcome with their Western partner, who has been seduced by the competitive game into making an attractive offer.

Stratagem prevention

People with whom conflict arises in your own camp should not be treated as the enemy. Instead, the focus should be placed on the common challenge faced jointly with these individuals. You should appeal to the reasoning that no one standing alone in their own camp can hold out against a strong opponent, and the only way to prevail is by coming together. Hence, strength-sapping internal trench warfare must be avoided. Anyone making a negative comment about another person within their own camp should provide evidence to support this. If individuals are discovered on your own side who "sleep in the same bed, but have different dreams," you should consider whether it would be better to get out of the bed or change your bed partner.

Stratagem risk

Special agents who are used may switch onto the opponent's side, thereby causing you damage, rather than bringing benefits.

Example

Thirty rather than thousands of sponsors

The Los Angeles Olympics were the first games to be run without government aid, yet this huge event generated a profit of $215 million. This was the achievement of games manager Peter Ueberroth, under whom the Olympic Games were fully commercialized for the first time. To begin with, he exploited the competition between different American television companies for the viewing rights, finally selling them to ABC for $225 million—a far higher price than had originally been expected. Thousands of businesses and companies wanted to act as sponsors, but, in order to curb the competition among them and achieve the maximum profit, Peter Ueberroth stipulated that only 30 companies, namely, one per branch of industry, would be accepted as sponsors. Each company had to donate a minimum of $4 million. In return, he offered sponsors the opportunity to decorate their products with Olympic symbols and sell them as "official" Olympic merchandise. In this way, he managed to earn more than $500 million simply by recruiting 30 sponsors (Chen 2, pp. 97–8).

Stratagem-linking

Stratagem 35:
The linking stratagem/Stratagem-linking

The formulation of this stratagem in the Chinese can be understood in two different ways.

1.   A stratagem linking different objects together. Linking stratagem.

2.   Different stratagems linked together. Stratagem-linking.

In accordance with the second interpretation, I have put this stratagem in a category of its own, that of stratagem-linking. Nevertheless, in its guise as a linking stratagem, stratagem 35 counts as an exploitation stratagem. Therefore, in this section, I will deal with both interpretations.

a.   Linking stratagem

1.   You defeat your opponent by tying one thing to another and, thus, incapacitating him:
     entangling stratagem.

2.   You skillfully link things together, especially contradictory elements:
     package stratagem.

b.   Stratagem-linking

To achieve your goal, you apply several stratagems at once, or one after the other.

To apply stratagem 35 as a linking stratagem, you can link together elements that influence your opponent, so that the latter is trapped or incapacitated by them, allowing you to win more easily. In the business world, however, it is frequently used as a package stratagem. In this guise, it is also useful as a tool for internal use, as it gives you an idea of how you can devise linking mechanisms, combined measures, sets of tactics and strategies, or a broader product spectrum, in order to achieve better results.

Stratagem-linking does not mean arbitrarily applying as many stratagems as possible. For, in general, the fewer stratagems you bind together, the better. Furthermore, in a specific situation, only a restricted number of stratagems is optimal. You should also have a clear idea of which stratagem is the most important, and of which stratagems you are only using to support it. Thus, you must grade your stratagems in order of importance, to avoid the danger that they could get in each other's way.

Stratagem radius

Entangling stratagem

In arms deals with certain countries, there are restrictions on the sales of important spare parts. This means that, once you have bought your weapons, if you need to buy any new spare parts later, you must either pay an inflated price for them, or make other concessions. Otherwise, there is a danger that your supplier will stop delivering your spare parts, and your weapons will not work (Yu 2003, pp. 176–7). In this case, the arms supplier has applied a linking stratagem, which also has elements of stratagem 28, using spare parts to form an inextricable bond with the buyer. This is similar to the bond allegedly formed between car dealers and buyers, when they sign restrictive contracts (*NZZ*, March 16, 2004, p. 46).

Package stratagem

Scientific studies have shown that people need approximately 50% more time to understand a negative answer than to understand an affirmative answer. Perhaps this is why a positive statement makes more impact on the addressee than a negative statement, if they are linked together. You can exploit this fact by applying a package stratagem. For example, in cigarette advertisements, you see a happy world of smokers in bright, joyous colors, and the compulsory health warning on the same billboard passes almost unnoticed.

A broad risk-spreading product spectrum is another practical application of this stratagem, as in the cases of Hitachi, whose products include both large electrical machines and domestic appliances, and General Electric, which produces both nuclear reactors and medical equipment. American fast-food chains have used stratagem 35 by combining simple food with a pleasant atmosphere and friendly service (Wee, p. 281). Some products are even charged with utopian associations, as in the case of the advertising slogan "New car, new happiness."

By skillfully joining things together, and carefully ranking contradictory things in order of their importance—for instance, by offering old, long-established products *and* new, constantly changing products at the same time—you can solve a number of problems. Take Chinese moon cake, for example. This is sold every fall in China, as part of a traditional festival, and people often buy it only because it comes in a beautiful box. In this instance, cake producers have subtly linked form and content. Chinese booksellers employ a similar piggyback sales technique, whereby you can only buy a best seller if you also buy a nonseller. Thus, they can get rid of the nonseller without slashing its price. In European countries, deals of this kind could be against the law.

In negotiations, you can make your opponent swallow a bitter pill, as long as you coat it in sugar. Or you can adopt the "carrot and stick" approach, one of Wu Xiangming's "management methods." He was the Shanghai Maglev Transportation Development Company's project leader responsible for building the Transrapid, a state-of-the-art railroad, and was also known as "Commander Wu" (*Süddeutsche Zeitung*, November 22/23, 2003, p. V1/1). One day, Wu learned that the wife of a German consultant with whom he had often clashed had fallen ill. Immediately, he stopped what he was doing, drove to a pharmacy, chose the best ginseng remedy available, had its instructions carefully translated, delivered it to the patient, and very carefully explained to her how to take it. The German consultant was quite overwhelmed by Wu Xiangming's gesture to his wife, since he knew how hectic Wu's schedule was. He realized that whenever Wu had come across as tough in their negotiations, it was obviously strictly business: There was no question of any personal hostility on his part (Zhu, p. 4). So by combining the "stick" used in negotiations with the "carrot" offered to the consultant's wife, Wu Xiangming clearly scored points with his German opponents and won their trust.

Firms can improve their image, and indirectly advertise their services, by linking their business activities with philanthropic or otherwise socially beneficial projects. In other words, they can link their "heads," that is, their cold economic rationality, with their "hearts," that is, their humanistic side.

Stratagem-linking

When applying stratagem 35, you can use two or more stratagems in a single action. The American theory of the "Chinese threat" is a good example of this, according to one Chinese author. First, this supposed menace scares the public at home, and they are happy to pay higher taxes to cover defense expenditure (stratagem 13). At the same time, it inflames the fears of the Taiwanese and China's other neighbors, prompting them to buy American weapons, thus strengthening the American military–industrial complex. America is particularly keen to aggravate tensions between Taiwan and China (stratagem 33). The same author draws the conclusion that, as a general rule, "America needs chaos (stratagem 20) and bloodshed (stratagem 5). A chaotic world is the foundation of America's good health. The fresh blood of America's enemies nourishes the flower of American freedom" (Yu 2003, p. 177).

Stratagem prevention

You can avoid being fooled by a package stratagem, as long as you realize in time that, although you are being offered what you want, it comes with strings attached. If these strings are completely unacceptable to you, then you should do without the thing you want. Most importantly, before committing yourself to anything, you must be careful. Package stratagems degenerate into package follies, if managers appear arrogant while pocketing million-dollar salaries.

If you can see that your opponent is using stratagem-linking against you, above all else, you must avoid falling victim to the first stratagem. Once you have been fooled by the first stratagem, it is generally difficult to avoid falling victim to the rest of them. For, "once you have embarked on the pirate ship, you are no longer your own master" (Yu 2003, p. 176). In many such cases, stratagem 36 is the most appropriate response: "[When the situation is gowing hopeless,] running away [in good time] is the best stratagem."

Examples

Package stratagem: No money left for management courses

Honeywell-Bull had virtually completed a deal with the Bank of China, when, suddenly, the Chinese clients' representative demanded a lower price. He claimed that, without it, he would lose face in the bank. The Honeywell-Bull manager replied that he could charge the lower price, but that, if he did, there would be no money left to train Chinese managers in America. So the Chinese delegation requested a short break. Having discussed the matter in private, the Chinese delegation accepted the original offer, and the deal was done. For the American had successfully applied a package stratagem: He had linked the reduction in price to something undesirable. Obviously, a trip to America was more appealing—in terms of pleasure and prestige—than a lower price (*HBR*, October 2003, p. 90).

Stratagem-linking: Transformation through trade

"Should we trade with China? Yes, we should, without reservation. Trade with China is a Trojan horse in which to transmit our ideas. It is not just the payment of a check for a shipment of grain" (*La Croix*, Paris, June 16, 1996, p. 16).

The Trojan horse was invented by Odysseus, the great Greek warrior. In order to end a protracted war with the Trojans, the Greeks created a gigantic horse out of wood, and some of their warriors hid in the horse's stomach. Then, leaving the wooden horse outside Troy's city walls, the Greek army pretended to retreat. In fact, it went and hid nearby on the seashore. The Trojans believed that the Greeks had withdrawn their forces, and, seeing the horse on the shore, they brought it into the city as a trophy of war. But by night, while they were asleep, the Greek warriors burst out of the horse's stomach, opened the gates of Troy, and gave a secret signal. By now, the army had returned from its hiding place, and, on receiving their signal, the soldiers attacked and occupied the city. Troy was defeated.

If we compare trade with China to a Trojan horse, we have two stratagems in mind.

Cloak-of-invisibility stratagem 1: "Crossing the sea while deceiving the heaven." The Greek vanguard entered the city of Troy without attracting the Trojans' attention. According to the same model, subversive ideas can enter China without attracting the attention of the Chinese. How can we achieve this? By trading with China. For trade offers us many opportunities to exchange ideas, to make personal contacts, and, in particular, to educate and influence Chinese personnel in Western countries. In the midst of all these economic contacts, subversive thoughts can pass unnoticed into the Middle Kingdom, possibly in the minds of Chinese personnel educated in the West. Like the Greek warriors hidden in the Trojan horse's belly, these inconspicuous but subversive ideas will overthrow the current regime.

Bait stratagem 17: "Tossing out a brick to attract jade." Trade with Western countries may be very interesting to the Chinese: Indeed, it may be indispensable to their efforts to modernize. But, from a Western perspective, we are merely throwing them a "brick." Compared to the "jade" that, eventually, we stand to gain as a result, we are making a minimal investment. For we expect the subversive side effects of trade to change the Chinese regime, in favor of a more liberal and democratic government.

It goes without saying that the Chinese have seen through such Western stratagemic calculation for a long time. They label it "peaceful evolution" and oppose it.

Stratagem-linking: The Transrapid saga

Thanks in no small part to opposition from the Greens, the Transrapid magnetic-suspension railroad project failed in Germany. Consequently, state-of-the-art German railroad technology enjoyed its world premiere as a commercial means of transportation not in its country of origin, but in China.[40]

As early as 1934, a German by the name of Hermann Kemper patented the magnetic-suspension railroad. In the sixties, the companies of Ludwig Bölkow and Krauss-Maffei constructed prototypes and demonstrated that they were viable. Moreover, in 1971, the German Ministry of Transportation financed a study, which recommended the development of a high-speed railroad. Various interests, however, prevented any further development. Officially, because the German national railroad had incurred a considerable debt, the German national railroad board and the German Ministry of Transportation decided to concentrate on modernizing conventional railroads, and all further research into the magnetic-suspension railroad was left to the German Ministry of Research. Here, they focused their attention on the technical aspects, but did nothing to have the magnetic railroad included in any German or European transportation plans. Here, the Germans failed to use the *kairos* stratagem, "[Quick-wittedly] leading away the sheep." They simply assumed that, because their technology was so advanced, it would be required sooner or later. This was obviously a "strategic error."[41]

By the time the Transrapid was finally ready, high-speed trains like the French TGV and Germany's own ICE left it without a niche to fill. Things appeared more hopeful in 1994, when the German government decided to have a Transrapid route built between Hamburg and Berlin, only to go back on this decision in 2000. Many now predicted the demise of the Transrapid project.[42] Thus, a means of transportation that had cost DM2 billion in taxpayers' money, spent on research, seemed finally to have crashed and burned.

The Chinese saw this German misfortune as an opportunity, and they took it (exploitation-of-need stratagem 5). Like a *deus ex machina*, Zhu Rongji, the Chinese prime minister, appeared on the scene. In June 2000, while on a state visit to Germany, he traveled on the test track in Lathen/Emsland. The technology made a great impression on him, and things started moving quickly from then on. In November of the same year, after the Chinese had conducted a feasibility study, negotiations began in Shanghai. Negotiations about the price were not easy. In fact, the whole project already looked like failing (blind-alley stratagem 28: "Removing the ladder after [the opponent] has climbed onto the roof"). *But then the German government promised to provide some of the funds, a decidedly positive development.*[43] On January 23, 2001, the city of Shanghai and Transrapid International signed a contract, committing them to building a 31.5-kilometer Transrapid track between Pudong Airport and downtown Shanghai. According to their contract, the Shanghai

Transrapid would cost DM1.293 billion: The Chinese had managed to halve the Germans' original asking price. They had achieved this, in part, by reducing the maximum permissible speed on the track from 505 to 430 kilometers per hour, thus undermining the German position (Zhu, p. 4) (incapacitation stratagem 19: "Removing the firewood from under the cauldron"). Furthermore, this was the first ever application of Transrapid technology worldwide, so Shanghai was suddenly the world leader in this field (Zhu, p. 4) (switch-position stratagem 18: "Catching the bandits by first catching the ringleader"). The train's eight components were delivered from Germany, as were the track switches and the components of the long-stator linear motor. The track, however, was built by the Chinese themselves, where the system originally intended for the German track was installed. These developments briefly rekindled interest in building short-distance magnetic-suspension railroads in Germany, but this interest soon died away again.

During a test run while the Transrapid was under construction, the extension cords of one of the magnetic motors overheated, suffering minor damage that was repaired fairly soon. ThyssenKrupp, one of the German firms, explained that a number of different factors had combined to cause minor damage in the cord insulation, adding that there had been no safety risk, and that the track was still in good working order. In spite of this, 3 of the 18 freight cars originally ordered were canceled, and *the Chinese started pressurizing Siemens and ThyssenKrupp, the two German contractors, into letting them produce more of the technology in China.* They applied *kairos* stratagem 12, "[Quick-wittedly] leading away the sheep," to take advantage of the faults in the German system. In the fall of 2003, Wu Xiangming, the project leader of the Shanghai Maglev Transportation Development Company, personally urged the head of Siemens, Heinrich von Pierer, *to transfer German technology to China,* including "essential patents that their German partners were understandably reluctant to hand over."[44] Here, the Chinese were preparing to apply stratagem 19, "Removing the firewood from under the cauldron." "The Chinese are forcing the Germans to get moving: unless the Transrapid is produced in China, they can see no prospect of any subsequent contracts."[45] (Here, they applied stratagem 17, "Tossing out a brick to attract jade": it was not clear what "subsequent contracts" they had in mind.) The Chinese justified the technology transfer on a number of grounds. They pointed out that they had first built their own magnetic railroad prototypes in the eighties, and that these could be developed further with German technology. The track system, which the Chinese had built using know-how bought in from a German company, had already undergone eight Chinese-patented improvements. These improvements solved problems of temperature fluctuation, movement of the concrete, and of the muddy ground in Shanghai.

The German contractors could guarantee that the system would work only as long as its reinforced concrete supports had no more than a tenth of a millimeter of tolerance. This degree of precision would be expensive, while, on the next sections of the track, costs— roughly €10 million per kilometer—*were due to be cut by 50%*. In response to this, about 100 engineers at the Maglev Research and Development Center, under the leadership of Fan Mo, were already working on an adapted "flexibility system" that would allow greater tolerance. This was a creeping application of hollowing-out stratagem 25, "Stealing the beams and replacing the pillars [on the inside, while leaving the facade of the house unchanged]."

Finally, the Chinese argued that the Transrapid's core technology had not moved on since the eighties. The Germans should now learn from the Chinese in Shanghai that new electronic developments should be more systematically applied to the system's electronic configuration. To put it mildly, the Chinese said, energy conservation on board the train itself was less than ideal, the air conditioning was suitable only for the German climate, and the interior design, seats, and noise levels left something to be desired.[46]

The Chinese already owned the track in Shanghai, which they had bought from the Germans and developed further. When the Germans visited the construction site, after a thorough inspection, they had frankly to admit that, "although Germany still had the best magnetic-suspension train technology, China was now the home of magnetic-suspension railroad-track technology" (Zhu, p. 4). This was due, in part, to an application of stratagem 19, "Removing the firewood from under the cauldron." "We must get used to the idea that the Chinese could apply for the contract to build the track in Germany," said Horst Fechner, director of BMG, the company responsible for the planned magnetic railroad track between Munich Airport and downtown Munich. Certainly, the Chinese would be the least expensive applicants, and the most experienced. The Germans are likely to suffer a similar fate when it comes to building the trains (incapacitation stratagem 19). Although ThyssenKrupp is still building trains in Kassel, it is only a matter of time before the Chinese scrutinize the German trains, "copy their technology and develop it further. In future, the Germans will only be partial suppliers of their own high-tech invention—and they will not even be using components produced in Germany. Even now, the Shanghai suspension railroad firm SMTDC gives lectures to prospective contractors about the future of the Transrapid, and the Germans do not even get a mention."[47]

When the first commercial Transrapid train made its maiden journey, the German celebrations were euphoric. They did not seem to realize that, really, they had "nothing to celebrate" at all.[48]

Escape stratagems

You can quickly and effectively get out of a tricky situation: stratagems 9, 11, 21, 36.

Stratagem 9:
Observing the fire burning on the opposite shore [seemingly uninvolved]

"Sitting on the mountain and watching the tigers fight." Especially if one is weak, one does not intervene in a crisis involving one's opponent, either to avoid getting embroiled in it oneself, or to reap the dividends later, when the situation changes to one's advantage (Chen 2, p. 93). This is a hybrid, a stratagem of both escape and exploitation.

Nonintervention stratagem; wait-and-see stratagem; stalling stratagem.

Stratagem radius

In the business world, you can imagine a situation where three people, A, B, and C, are aiming for the same goal. A and B are equally well qualified; C is not so well qualified, and is surely doomed to fail. A bitter rivalry develops between A and B, while C calmly stands back and does not get involved. So A and B lay into each other, until they have canceled each other out. What is more, they have been discredited for fighting. Who will reach the goal? C, of course, despite having been the weakest candidate. This is not because C was better qualified than the other two: It is because, thanks to the use of stratagem 9, C never looked bad (Chen 2, p. 93). People who employ stratagem 9 in everyday life in China are accused of cowardice. If they see something bad happening, they will avoid getting involved, so that they are not affected by it.

Stratagem prevention

One should not thoughtlessly let the public know about internal problems: otherwise, everyone will see the "fire burning," and your opponents will take their opportunity to "loot the burning house," that is, to use stratagem 5.

Stratagem risk

If you "observe the fire" on the other shore and do nothing, you may pay very dearly for your inactivity if the fire spreads to your side. Hence, it is not good enough simply to watch the fire burning. You have to take other safety measures.

Example

Building ships during a drought

There is an ancient Chinese saying, "Build ships in a drought, and wagons in the event of a flood." Normal commercial logic dictates the exact opposite: You build wagons in a drought, and ships in the event of a flood, since there is a demand for wagons in a drought, and a demand for ships in the event of a flood. This old saying, however, takes account of the vagaries of the market, and encourages a longer-term perspective. As the proverb has it, "The fool is earning today: The wise man will earn tomorrow" (Zhang, p. 44). You should look beyond the immediate market situation to the opposite shore, take note of the "fire" of future consumer needs, and adjust your business strategy accordingly. For droughts and floods will assuredly come and go, and if you produce only wagons during the droughts and ships during the floods, then you will get into difficulties. Though profitable in the short term, your business will go up in smoke as soon as the market changes. If, on the other hand, you take into account how the market will change after the drought or the flood, then you will prosper.

Stratagem 11:

Letting the plum tree wither in place of the peach tree

You save your own skin, or someone else's, and, in so doing, you let someone else take the responsibility. With or without their knowledge or consent, someone is designated as the fall guy. You eliminate a peripheral character, so as to save the skin of an important one. In order to shift the responsibility, you can also blame things or facts: "tradition," "the spirit of the age," "globalization," "the facts," "the press," "the market," "the devil," "the stars," that sort of thing. Chinese government officials blame their own mistakes on "red-tape," meaning that they personally are not to blame: It is the fault of something more general and intangible (*Workers' Daily*, Beijing, February 9, 1988, p. 2).

Scapegoat or sacrificial-lamb stratagem.

In a more abstract sense, this stratagem's goal is to make a substantial profit by accepting a comparatively minor loss. It is, as such, a hybrid stratagem, a means of both escape and exploitation. It is the sacrifice of something unimportant in order to gain something important; the surrender of a tactical advantage in order to achieve a strategic victory; the sacrifice of a part to preserve the whole.

Fall-guy stratagem.

Stratagem radius

One way of applying this stratagem is to limit the blame for any inappropriate conduct to those directly responsible. This obviates any consideration of wider responsibility, and preserves the culprits' superiors, as well as the company itself, and any of its structural or organizational inadequacies, from any share of the blame. So it was that all the crimes committed during the Chinese Cultural Revolution (1966–1976) were blamed on the so-called Gang of Four, thus saving Mao Zedong's tarnished reputation. In the People's Republic of China, criticism is always very carefully directed at "individual people" and "individual phenomena" (*gebie xianxiang*): The political system itself is never actually denounced.

The late Pope John Paul II apologized for crimes committed by Catholics in the past, but claimed that only individual Christians were to blame. Thus, he endeavored to present the Church as a body that could not be held accountable for the "sinful behavior of its members" (*NZZ*, August 11, 2000, p. 54). In other words, the whole was untainted by the sins of the parts, and the Church emerged in the best possible light. Arthur Andersen's attorneys adopted the same approach to the Enron scandal, claiming that "the misconduct of *individual members* in the Houston office—where most of the files were destroyed—did not justify the prosecution of the entire firm" (*NZZ*, March 15, 2002, p. 21).

In the late seventies, China justified the liberalization of its *foreign-trade policy* to the Chinese public by presenting it as a shrewd application of stratagem 11, though it was never explicitly described as such. They used quotations from Lenin about the "New Economic Policy" of the Soviet Union. He said that the Soviet economy could not be rebuilt without technical assistance from capitalist countries; that any agreements with capitalist countries would have to be subject to very tight controls; but that, in order to receive any foreign help, the Soviets would have to allow the capitalists to make their profits. He made these concessions in order to make a far greater gain, in the guise of a strong Soviet economy (*Strategeme 1*, 11.18).

The West German national soccer team also employed stratagem 11 in their *victorious 1954 World Cup* in Bern, Switzerland. In their group game against Hungary, the West German coach, Sepp Herberger, left seven first-choice players on the sidelines. His weakened side was humiliated, losing 8–3. This is a pretty spectacular defeat in a soccer game, but it meant that the rested players had a huge physical advantage over Austria in the semifinal, as the Austrians were exhausted after their dramatic 7–5 victory over the Swiss in the previous round. The Germans cruised to a 6–1 victory, and went on to meet Hungary again in the final (*NZZ*, November 7, 2003, p. 58), which they won 3–2.

Stratagem prevention

Either one must avoid getting into a precarious situation—in which one may have to take the blame for someone else's mistake—in the first place, or one must act quickly to get out of it. By careful global analysis, one can avoid responsibility being shifted onto an individual scapegoat.

Stratagem risk

"A study shows that managers are very rarely self-critical. They act as if they were made of Teflon: Nothing ever sticks. Other people are always to blame. It is only human to try and shift the blame onto factors beyond your control; but, in a rescue operation, this is a fatal mistake" (*Handelsblatt*, August 22/23, 2003). If you let things get so bad that you can only employ stratagem 11 to save your skin, then you are in pretty serious trouble. There is a risk that no "plum tree" can be found. If you panic and look for a scapegoat, rather than conducting an honest review of your situation, your business will surely fail. Why not be a bit more cunning, and act as a "whipping boy" yourself? (See stratagem 34.)

Examples

Iacocca's plum trees

The contemporary American cult of famous and successful CEOs started with Lee Iacocca (1924–1999). His use of stratagem 11, as chair and CEO of the Chrysler Corporation, was particularly ingenious. He was appointed in 1979, and he spent the following years conducting "one of the largest clean-up operations in the history of the American car industry" (*CM*, p. 1323). Among other things, he introduced severe cost-cutting measures, reduced surplus stock, and significantly downsized his workforce. These were the "plum trees" he sacrificed (Yu 1994, pp. 83–4) to save his "peach tree": A mere four years after his appointment, Chrysler made an annual profit of more than $900 million.

100,000 pairs of lost shoes

In 1984, Mr. Sato, who was on the board of a Japanese commercial company, bought 100,000 faultless shoes from a Chinese shoe manufacturer, and had them transported to Japan. Unfortunately, the shoes did not make much of an impression, and Sato's company was stuck with them. So he went back to China in person to ask for help. After a week, the Chinese told him that they would replace all the old shoes with 100,000 new shoes, all with a new design. He returned to Japan a happy man. The new consignment of shoes arrived as promised, and the company's PR campaign for the new shoes put a great deal of emphasis on the Chinese supplier's excellent service. Fortunately, this time around, the shoes were a hit with the public. The following year, the Japanese ordered 300,000 pairs; in 1988, they ordered no fewer than 1.5 million pairs. Thus, the Chinese successfully applied stratagem 11: "The manufacturer gave away 100,000 pairs, so that it could eventually sell 1.5 million" (Yu 1994, p. 84).

The generous soybean buyer

Soybean seller V's asking price was $150 per (metric) ton, but buyer K offered only $136 per ton. Then V lowered the price to $145, but K refused to go above $140, so no deal was made. Suddenly, three days later, V saw that he would soon have some serious financial problems, and it seemed a very good idea to make a quick sale to K. Thus, V telephoned K and offered him the soybeans for $140 per ton. During the new negotiations, V was also totally open with K about his financial problems. After careful consideration, K informed V that he would not only buy the soybeans, but would pay $145 per ton. V was delighted and astonished: He could not believe his luck! Later, someone asked K's negotiator why he had paid a higher price than he had to. He replied that he had bought only 3,000 tons at the higher price, and so had lost only $15,000. This was a trivial amount from K's perspective, and a sacrifice well worth making, since it would guarantee excellent relations with K's supplier in future. Sure enough, both companies, K and V, worked very closely together from then on, and V would frequently offer K special deals and privileges. "Thus, the loss of $15,000 on one day was as nothing compared to the ensuing long-term gain" (Yu 1994, pp. 90–1).

Using the plum-tree stratagem when negotiating deals

If you must make concessions—or sacrifice plum trees—do not start your negotiations by making any important sacrifices.

Make a single concession: Sacrifice a single plum tree, and do not make it too big. Concessions are best made in small quantities. Never give up a single plum tree without a fight. Make your opponent sweat for every single tree you sacrifice, and make sure you have something from them in return. You can also sacrifice the odd fake plum tree—make what look like concessions, but which really cost you nothing. Always make sure you know what your final concession is going to be, because the last one you make is the most important one.

Stratagem 21:

The cicada casts off its skin of gleaming gold

金
蟬
脫
殼

When a larva becomes an adult cicada, it slips out of its skin, which appears to gleam like gold in the sunlight, and escapes unnoticed, while its pursuers are distracted by the skin of gleaming gold left behind. In general, you employ this stratagem to escape from danger (Zhou 1992, p. 61). In one sense, it is a specific variant of stratagem 36, or "running away" (Lin, p. 30), and, to this extent, it is an escape stratagem. But the change of appearance can serve other purposes (Yu 2003, p. 122). For example, you can use it in order to apply stratagem 1, "Crossing the sea while deceiving the heaven," like a spy posing as a businessperson, or a police officer going undercover as a drug dealer. In the business world, stratagem 21 can also be used offensively, for example, to improve your position in the market (Lin, p. 122).

There are numerous ways to apply this stratagem, two of which are outlined below.

1. Distract your opponent from your escape, whether by making a simple statement, for example, "I need to use the bathroom," or by improvising a showpiece. This "escape" can be understood in an abstract as well as a physical sense. For instance, in China, legal proceedings that discharge people from liability are seen as applications of this stratagem.
    Evasion stratagem.

2. The cicada casts off its skin in order to assume a different form, so that it has more room for maneuver.
    Metamorphosis stratagem.

Stratagem radius

Evasion stratagem

In the thirties, a Shanghai speculator called Zhao suggested to a banker called Du that they set up a trade consortium using extremely unstable government loans. Within two days, Zhao needed 4 million Chinese dollars in cash. Du thought to himself: "This guy is scared. He has miscalculated in his speculations, and now he is in trouble, because he will soon have to pay his dues. He is using the consortium, which he suggested setting up, to stall and distract his creditors. For who is going to think that a man who could set up such a powerful consortium is going to be short of funds? They will not demand to be paid right on time. They will let him put them off, and he will not have to make any immediate payments. He is not using that old stratagem, 'The cicada casts off its skin of gleaming gold,' is he?" Du conjectured that Zhao was, indeed, using stratagem 21. You can read more of this story of intrigue in the Chinese business world, in a novel by Mao Dun (1896–1981).[49]

Stratagem 21 sometimes entails cleverly talking your way out of trouble. "Come on! We're only human! We're not machines! People make mistakes!" Irrespective of what you have done wrong, you can use these lines to take the heat off you. In fact, you can apply stratagem 21 as a means of self-justification if you are directly criticized. Simply focus everyone's attention on some minor mistake to which you confess, and you will buy time to cover up any serious misconduct on your part (Yu 1993, p. 204).

In large organizations, you can spread the blame across an entire hierarchy, effectively granting immunity to everyone in it. For example, a bridge collapsed in Portugal, killing 59 people, but an inquest found no one guilty of anything (*NZZ*, March 26, 2004, p. 19).

Metamorphosis stratagem

Ma Ji, a Chinese comedian, performed a sketch on Central Chinese Television as part of its 1983 New Year program, which was broadcast throughout the country. Here, he ridiculed misleading advertisements, referring to the PR campaign for "Universum," an imaginary brand of cigarettes. The sketch was broadcast at the best time of year for ratings, and was a huge comic success. But Wang Zhengzhen, the director of a tobacco company in the province of Heilongjiang, was not only amused: He was galvanized into action. On the one hand, the comedian had made fun of Universum; on the other hand, the brand name was on everyone's lips. Wang reckoned that he could cash in on this. Immediately, he set up a working group to create a Universum cigarette, which they produced that same year. Right from the outset, Universum cigarettes were in great demand, which Wang increased further by using Ma Ji, the comedian, himself in the advertising campaign, and by continually improving the quality of the product. In spite of fierce competition in the Chinese cigarette market, Universum gained a rock-solid position. Its manufacturer had already had a cigarette on the market, but it had not made much of an impression. By subtly shedding the old brand name and rebranding the original product with a name that everyone already knew without any advertising, Wang Zhengzhen applied stratagem 21 quite brilliantly (Chen 2, p. 220).

When China first liberalized its foreign-trade policy, in spite of their high quality, its exports were largely ignored by foreign businesspeople. Subsequently, Chinese manufacturers realized why this was: their packaging was too drab. Now, dull packaging had had no adverse effect on product sales in the Chinese market, as long as the economy was state-controlled. It would, however, get Chinese products absolutely nowhere in the world market. As soon as Chinese manufacturers recognized this, their products cast off their old skin and slipped into new, attractive packaging, and, at last, they started selling well in foreign markets (Yu 1994, pp. 171ff.).

When America entered World War I, one major beneficiary was Boeing Airplane Company, whose products were suddenly in great demand: the Marines ordered 50 seaplanes. But, after the end of the war, new government contracts failed to materialize, and the future looked bleak. So William Boeing (1881–1956) decided to do something about it. Without losing sight of opportunities in the military aircraft market—so as not to lose it to the competition— Boeing concentrated on producing commercial civil airliners. Following the success of this venture, he went into airmail transportation (CM, p. 1225 ff). His timely shift of emphasis from an unprofitable line to more profitable ones, without totally abandoning the unprofitable, and his careful preparation for possible future scenarios, were both successful applications of stratagem 21 (Chen 1, pp. 221–2; Wee, pp. 169–70).

Stratagem prevention

Whenever your opponent is really trying to focus your attention on something, do not be fooled.

Stratagem risk

If the "skin" you cast off is too inconspicuous, if it does not gleam like gold, and fails to attract anyone's attention, then this stratagem will be exposed.

Examples

Saved by bankruptcy

The most influential daily newspaper in China accused the authorities of using the "cicada casts off its skin of gleaming gold" stratagem in order to exonerate state-owned companies from their debts. The authorities let these companies abruptly declare themselves bankrupt, and had subsequently registered them under different names. Thus, it was much more difficult to recover the companies' debts, since they were now officially defunct (*RR*, August 20, 1997, p. 9). What the Chinese needed stratagem 21 to achieve, we can "legitimately" do in the West, just so long as it is not a delayed or fraudulent declaration of bankruptcy. Within limits, stratagem 21 has effectively been legalized. One excellent example of stratagem 21 in action is the WorldCom scandal. WorldCom collapsed with huge debts; but on April 20, 2004, it emerged from bankruptcy proceedings with a new name, MCI. As part of its clean-up operation, as required by Chapter 11 of American bankruptcy law, the books from 2000 to 2002 were altered by $73.7 billion. About $35 billion in debts was written off. Most WorldCom creditors received 36% of their repayments in the form of new stocks and obligations. Its stockholders, who had had $180 billion to their names at the height of the stock-market boom, were left with practically nothing. By the end of the bankruptcy proceedings, MCI owed just $5.5 billion in debts ("Phönix aus der Asche: WorldCom tritt aus dem Konkursverfahren" ["Phoenix from the ashes: WorldCom emerges from bankruptcy proceedings"], *NZZ*, April 21, 2004, p. 21).

Avoiding blame when negotiations fail

Sometimes, when the Chinese have decided that they can no longer do business with someone, they will make demands that cannot be met, leaving the other party with no choice but to reject them. Thus, they cannot be blamed for the ensuing breakdown of negotiations (Fang, p. 270).

Stratagem 36:

[When the situation is growing hopeless,] running away [in good time] is the best stratagem

走
爲
上

Life is never exclusively a matter of victories: It is made up of many minor triumphs and defeats. In business as in war, you very rarely need only to win one battle. You should aim not primarily for tactical victories in small skirmishes, but for a conclusive strategic victory, possibly after a number of tactical defeats. Never running away during a strategic encounter does not make you heroic; nor does strategically running away make you a coward (Chen 2, p. 362). "A good fighter is not ashamed to run away," said the son of Ts'ao Ts'ao, one of the protagonists in the era of the Three Kingdoms (AD 220–280). Only those who can lose can also win (Yu 2003, p. 183). Nevertheless, "standing your ground" and "running away" have to be carefully weighed against each other, and you must always choose the right time to run away (Chen 1, p. 365).

Stubbornness can lead you down a blind alley. If you can see a hopeless situation looming on the horizon, then it is only right to retreat in time rather than pointlessly wasting your energy. In the worst-case scenario, "running away" becomes simply a means of escape (Yu 2003, p. 178), but this stratagem can be used more artfully as a timely, calculated change of position, with a tactical or strategic goal in mind (Zhou 1992, p. 114; Yu 2003, p. 178). A timely retreat from an opponent whom you cannot yet defeat allows you both to preserve your strength and to keep your options open: You may even be able to make a comeback. To apply this stratagem in a crisis, however, you need to make sure in advance that there is an emergency exit, and a place where you can take refuge. You must choose this place in advance and with care.

Retreat stratagem; change-of-course stratagem; getaway stratagem.
You can also use this stratagem without a direct opponent, if you are faced with a task beyond your abilities. When you have achieved your greatest success, before your efforts inevitably go downhill, stratagem 36 can give you more options. It can also be applied when you have nothing more to win but a lot to lose, or, in another scenario, if you cannot avoid being exposed, but want to take precautions to avoid taking full responsibility for your possible failure, and paying the ultimate price.

Distancing-yourself stratagem.
You should always be prepared for your business to become obsolete. Right from the outset, you should realize that business models can become dated, and you should be prepared to "run away" to more profitable business models. In delicate undertakings, you must always have an emergency exit available. Moreover, if you must make any predictions or other statements about something you are unclear about, make them vague enough for you not to be tied down. Sometimes, it is helpful to link stratagem 20, "Clouding the water to catch the fish [robbed of their clear sight]" (making imprecise statements), to stratagem 36. Ambivalent "on the one hand, on the other hand" behavior, and oracular pronouncements, can give you a wider range of options in future, and steer you clear of blind alleys. Making clear statements, only to distort them later or claim that they were misunderstood, is certainly a mistake to avoid.

Stratagem radius

In the business world, firms apply stratagem 36 by retreating from difficult areas of business and entering new ones, while company owners who can see the writing on the wall for their line of business apply this stratagem by retiring (Chen 2, p. 365). Companies also apply it by abandoning a tactic or strategy that no longer works, or by dropping a product if it seems likely to be outstripped by the competition. In addition, some firms avoid confronting their competitors where the latter have a strong presence, and go into areas where they show signs of weakness. This is so that they can establish a strong market position with original products, and is another application of stratagem 36 (Zhou 1992, p. 114). After World War II, the American mainstream beer market was dominated by the leading domestic brands, so foreign brewers like Heineken went into areas where the competition was less daunting, like the imported beer market, in which they became market leaders (Yao, pp. 293ff.). If it proves difficult to enter a market, it is best to withdraw from it, if only for the time being. Kentucky Fried Chicken (KFC) can vouch for this. In the late sixties, it tried to establish a position in the Asian market, opening restaurants in Hong Kong. However, at that time, Hong Kong was not yet ready for fast food, so, instead of persevering, KFC decided to withdraw. Not that it had given up on Asia: After a while, KFC outlets opened in Singapore, where they enjoyed greater success. From its experiences in Hong Kong and Singapore, KFC learned that it was best to market its product not as a mere fast-food snack, but as a modern lifestyle symbol. Its success in Singapore gave it a second chance to enter Hong Kong, and now it also has a strong position on the Chinese mainland (Wee, p. 287).

You can use stratagem 36 to avoid paying bribes. Instead of making rather undignified monetary transactions or offering gifts, you can employ alternatives that make good business sense. For example, you can provide samples of your products, subsidize scholarships at foreign universities, or offer further training courses in your Western mother company. Of course, whenever you present such inducements, you should ensure that you are both ethically and legally covered, and that you have a way out, should it be required.

In some cases, this stratagem allows ailing firms to merge with other firms, or to join a consortium (Yu 1994, pp. 314–15).

In accordance with stratagem 36, you should include a number of clauses in the fine print of your insurance contracts, detailing a wide range of scenarios that are not covered.

There are few better exponents of the art of "running away" than the French president, Jacques Chirac. Asked by a woman journalist about the ambitious politician Nicolas Sarkozy, he looked at her neckline and replied, "That's a nice necklace you're wearing." When the lady persisted, saying, "Sure, but what about Sarkozy?" again he pretended not to hear, replying, "Is your necklace from the Antilles?" And when the journalist tried to ask him a third time, he interrupted her and remarked, "Ah, the Antilles are beautiful" (*Der Spiegel*, no. 5, 2004, p. 157). In this instance, Chirac's successful application of stratagem 36 was helped by stratagem 27.

Stratagem prevention

Lawmakers should establish a legal order that does not force the economy to "run away" from taxation, or from anything else. If your opponent uses stratagem 36 in a negotiation, you should not let it scare you. You should focus not on the fact that they have "run away," but assume that they have an ulterior motive. You can also tell your opponent to put all their cards on the table, so that they cannot resort to this stratagem. Before you sign a contract with anyone, you must ensure that they have not used stratagem 20, that is, there must be no vaguely worded clauses that give them a way out.

Stratagem risk

It is possible to "run away" too soon. As a result, you could miss out on a favorable situation.

Example

"Excuse me, but I have other things to do"

In July 1984, a Chinese delegation began negotiations with the representative of a Tunisian firm, with a view to constructing a fertilizer factory on a particularly favorable site, in the port of Ch'in-huang-tao. After several rounds, all of which went very smoothly, a third party joined the negotiations in October 1984. He was the chair of a Kuwaiti firm, and a very experienced and resolute man. Once he learned what had been verbally agreed between the Chinese and the Tunisians, he declared, "Everything you have discussed so far is worthless. We must start these negotiations again." Both the Chinese and the Tunisians were deeply unhappy with this. The feasibility study alone had cost $200,000, and they had employed more than ten experts over three months. It clearly made no sense to start the whole process again. Yet no one dared to say this to his face. His appearance was too forbidding, and only the oil minister outranked him in the Kuwaiti hierarchy. Moreover, he was the chair of an international fertilizer company, and the firm that he was representing owned a large number of stocks in Tunisian firms. The atmosphere in the conference room was almost unbearable. Then the Chinese local government representative stood up and said, "We have already prepared a plot on which to build this factory, in an ideal location near the port. Many joint ventures want the legal right to use this plot, and we have turned them all down. If we agree to the Kuwaiti chair's suggestion and continue to delay this project, then we will have no choice but to give the plot to someone else. Excuse me, but I have other things to do. I hereby declare that I am withdrawing from these negotiations." Whereupon he took his briefcase and left the room. A Chinese official rushed after him to persuade him to come back; but he just smiled at him mischievously and said, "I'm not going away. I'm just going to wait in another room. I have no doubt that the next stage in the negotiations will go very smoothly." The local government representative had been waiting in the adjoining room for just half an hour, when a Chinese subordinate came running in to tell him that everything had worked out for the best. It was the issue of the plot that had influenced the Kuwaiti chair: He wanted to make absolutely sure that they would be able to use it for their project.

Just as the Chinese local government representative had anticipated, negotiations ran like clockwork from then on, the three parties soon agreed terms, and the contract was signed. From this account, one Chinese author draws the conclusion that stratagem 36 can be used to end a stalemate at a critical stage in a negotiation, and to soften your opponent's hard-line stance. Nevertheless, you must use this stratagem at the right moment, and—should the situation arise—you must back it up with something extra to lower your opponent's resistance. This stratagem should be employed mostly against hostile, uncooperative negotiators. You should not use it if your opposite number's intentions are benign. In addition, you should contemplate exactly how you are going to apply the stratagem in a negotiation, and what measures to take once you have applied it. Thus, you ensure that you always remain in control. Obviously, the application of stratagem 36 can go wrong, and may even lead to a breakdown in negotiations. You should think very carefully about this before taking such a risk (Yu 1994, pp. 317ff.).

Conclusion

More than 50 books linking the 36 stratagems with the themes of economic warfare and business leadership have been published in China and Taiwan over the last 15 years. Faced with such an abundance of literature dealing with Chinese stratagems and their applications in economics and management, Western leaders cannot afford to bury their heads in the sand. They should study this source of wisdom in depth, although it is almost unknown in Western circles, and, within ethical limits, they should take full advantage of it—and not only when doing business with the Chinese. Hence, this book is by no means simply the result of some Western author's bright idea. Faced with global demands, we need to respond by thinking beyond the limits of European thought. As far as this author is aware, this is the first Western publication for Western economic leaders based on the evaluation and systematic analysis of a representative selection of books written in Chinese (and not available in any other language) on the use of the 36 stratagems in economics and management.

According to Leibniz (1646–1716), China is, "as it were, a Europe of the East," and is "above us in some respects, beneath us in others." When it comes to "the rules governing human interaction," we are "surpassed by the Chinese." Western countries may be wiser than the Chinese, as far as normal human interaction is concerned. For example, European nations are keen to encourage the Chinese to adopt the rule of law. But when it comes to non-conventional cunning human behavior, China is ahead of Europe. It would be a good idea to catch up with China in this respect. Europeans, particularly managers, should know what the Chinese know about trickery, and should use it, so long as they do so ethically. European managers could learn from Master Sun, and try to adapt, like running water. "Just as running water avoids the heights and rushes into the depths, an army steers clear of the strong and attacks the weak. Just as water always flows in different ways, depending on the obstacles it encounters, an army always triumphs in a different way, depending on the enemy. Just as water does not exist in a fixed state, nothing is always the same for an army." But a flexible approach cannot be exploited to the full, if you approach your situation in a conventional way. Unless you understand stratagems, your assessment of situations and your ability to use them are bound to be impaired, and you cannot avoid the danger that the Confucian philosopher Mencius (372–289 BC) warns us against: "All cleverness and wisdom are in vain if you do not know how to use your situation, just as the plough and the axe achieve nothing if they are not used at the right time." Finally, however, managers should follow Jesus' advice and combine the shrewdness of the snake with the innocence of the dove. They should also heed the warning of the Chinese sage Hong Zicheng: "You must not have a heart that harms people! But a heart that is wary of people is indispensable!"

Abbreviations and Bibliography

B	*Bild*, German daily newspaper
Brahm	Laurence J. Brahm, *Negotiating in China: 36 Strategies*, 2nd ed., Hong Kong 1996
BZ	*Basler Zeitung*, Swiss daily newspaper
C	*Cash*, Zurich-based Swiss weekly newspaper
Chen 1	Chen Caijun, *Sanshiliu Ji Yu Qiye Guanli* [*The 36 Stratagems and Enterprise Management*], Lanzhou 2003
Chen 2	Chen Caijun, *Sanshiliu Ji Yu Shangzhan Zhimou* [*The 36 Stratagems: A Wealth of Ideas in the Business War*], 2nd ed., Lanzhou 2003
CM	*Campus Management*, Frankfurt/New York 2003 (originally published in English under the title *Business*, Bloomsbury Publishing Plc, 2002)
Fang	Tony Fang, *Chinese Business Negotiating Style: A Socio-Cultural Approach*, Linköping 1997
Feng	Feng Liangnu, *Sanshiliu Ji Sun Zi Bingfa Shangzhan Qishi Lu* [*The 36 Stratagems and Master Sun's Art of War: Inspirational Notes for the Business War*], Beijing 2000
FAZ	*Frankfurter Allgemeine Zeitung*, German daily newspaper
FS	*Falü yu Shenghuo* [*Law and Life*], Chinese monthly magazine, Beijing
FTD	*Financial Times Deutschland*, German-language version of the *Financial Times*
Fu	Fu Wenzhang and Fu Yingquan, *Sanshiliu Ji Yu Xiandai Shichang Jingji* [*The 36 Stratagems and the Modern Market Economy*], Beijing 2001
HBM	*Harvard Business Manager*, Hamburg
HBR	*Harvard Business Review*, Boulder, Colorado

Jullien   François Jullien, *Über die Wirksamkeit* [*A Treatise on Efficacy*], Berlin 1999

Küng   Hans Küng, *Kleine Geschichte der katholischen Kirche* [*A Brief History of the Catholic Church*], 3rd ed., Berlin 2003

KdL   Harro von Senger, *Die Kunst der List* [*The Art of Cunning*], 4th ed., Munich 2004

Larousse   Pierre Larousse, *Grand dictionnaire universel du XIXe siècle*, nineteenth-century French dictionary, Parties neuves, tome treizième, Paris 1875

Li   Li Guangdou, *Shangzhan Bingfa Xin 36 Ji Quanshu* [*The Art of War for the Business War: A New Compendium of the 36 Stratagems*], Beijing 2002

Lin   Lin Bin, *Shangzhan Sanshiliu Ji* [*The 36 Stratagems in the Business War*], Taipei 1995

List   Harro von Senger (ed.), *Die List* [*Cunning*], 4th ed., Frankfurt 2003

Mauch   Ulrich Mauch, *Jesus und die List: Über menschenfreundliche Strategeme* [*Jesus and Cunning: On Philanthropic Stratagems*], 2nd ed., Zurich 2001

NZZ   *Neue Zürcher Zeitung*, Swiss daily newspaper

QXS   *Quanguo Xin Shumu* [*National Catalog of New Books*], Chinese monthly magazine, Beijing

RR   *Renmin Ribao* [*People's Daily*], Chinese daily, Beijing

RRH   *Renmin Ribao Haiwaiban* [*People's Daily, Overseas Issue*], Chinese daily, Beijing

Strategeme 1   Harro von Senger, *Strategeme Band 1* [*Stratagems*, vol. 1], 12th ed., Munich 2003

Strategeme 2   Harro von Senger, *Strategeme Band 2* [*Stratagems*, vol. 2], 3rd ed., Munich 2004

SZ   *SonntagsZeitung*, Zurich-based Swiss weekly newspaper

TA   *Tages-Anzeiger*, Zurich-based Swiss daily newspaper

Wee   Wee Chou Hou and Lan Luh Luh, *The 36 Strategies of the Chinese: Adapting Ancient Chinese Wisdom to the Business World*, Singapore 2003

Wei   Wei Chiyun, *Sanshiliu Ji: Zhongguoren de Zhimou* [*The 36 Stratagems: The Resourcefulness of the Chinese*], Taipei 1992

WW   *Die Weltwoche*, Zurich-based Swiss weekly magazine

Yan   Yan Jiazhen et al., *Fan Sanshiliu Ji* [*Opposing the 36 Stratagems*], 2nd ed., Beijing 1996

Yao   Yao Siyuan, *Sanshiliu Ji: Chaoji Shangzhan Celüe* [*The 36 Stratagems: Clever Courses of Action in the Business Super War*], Taipei 1997

Ye   Ye Zi, *Sanshiliu Ji Yu Zhimou Jingshang* [*The 36 Stratagems and Resourceful Business Leadership*], Beijing 2002

Yu 1993   Yu Xuebin, *Sanshiliu Ji Xin Jie Xiang Xi* [*The 36 Stratagems: New Explanations and In-Depth Analysis*], Beijing 1993

Yu 1994   Yu Chujie, *Shangyong Sanshiliu Ji* [*The 36 Stratagems for Business Use*], Wuhan 1994

Yu 2003   Yu Rubo, *Da Hua Sanshiliu Ji* [*A Comprehensive Discussion of the 36 Stratagems*], Jinan 2003

Yuan   Yuan Shijun et al., *Bingfa Yu Shangzhan* [*The Art of War and Business War*], Beijing 1992

Zhang   Zhang Yongjun, *Manhua 36 Ji Shangzhan Xin Shuo* [*New Illustrated Guide to the 36 Stratagems in the Business War*], Taipei 2002

Zhou 1992   Zhou Yuxiang, *Sanshiliu Ji Yingyong Zhinan* [*Guide to Using the 36 Stratagems*], Beijing 1992

Zhou 1993   Zhou Junquan, Ge Zhonglun, and Zhou Gang, *Shangzhan 36 Ji: Shili Jingxuan* [*The 36 Stratagems in the Business War: An Exquisite Collection of Practical Examples*], Shijiazhuang 1993

Zhu   Zhu Jinchen and Yu Zhicheng, "Jiayu shijian de ren: Ji Shanghai cifu gongcheng zongzhihui Wu Xiangming"

["The man who is master of time: Notes about Wu Xiangming, project leader of the Shanghai magnetic railroad project"], *Wenxue Bao* [*Literature Newspaper*], Shanghai, January 9, 2003

ZQB　　*Zhongguo Qingnian Bao* [*Chinese Youth Newspaper*], daily, Beijing

Notes

1 Carl von Clausewitz, *Vom Kriege* [On War], Drittes Buch: Von der Strategie überhaupt [Book Three: On Pure Strategy], Abschnitt X: Die List [Section X: Cunning], edited by Wolfgang Pickert and Wilhelm Ritter von Schramm, 2nd ed., Pfaffenhofen 1969, p. 107.

2 *Zhongguo Funü* [Chinese Woman], Beijing, no. 11, 1996, p. 32.

3 Johann Gottfried von Herder, "Von Nothwendigkeit und Nutzen der Schulen" ["On the necessity and use of schools"], 1783, quoted in Thomas Neumann (ed.), *Quellen zur Geschichte Thüringens: Pädagogik im 18. und 19. Jahrhundert* [Sources of the History of Thüringen: Education in the Eighteenth and Nineteenth Centuries], Center for Political Education, Erfurt 2002, pp. 84–5.

4 For this information, I would like to thank Dr. Manfred M. Frühauf, LSI-Sinicum, Bochum. Information received on March 24, 2004.

5 Eberhard Schockenhoff, "List und Lüge in der theologischen Tradition" ["Cunning and lies in the theological tradition"], in *List*, p. 160.

6 Stuart Crainer, *Die 75 besten Managemententscheidungen aller Zeiten* [The 75 Greatest Management Decisions Ever Made], Vienna/ Frankfurt 2000, p. 7.

7 Kaihan Krippendorff, *The Art of Advantage*, New York 2003, p. xv.

8 Niccolò Machiavelli, *Der Fürst* [The Prince], translated, introduced, and annotated by Friedrich Blaschke, Leipzig 1924, pp. 26, 109.

9 Wu Cheng'en, *La Pérégrination vers l'Ouest I* [*Journey to the West*, vol. 1], Paris 1991, pp. 390–3.

[10] Clausewitz, *Vom Kriege*, p. 108.

[11] Xue Guo'an, *"Sunzi Bingfa" Yu "Zhanzheng Lun" Bijiao Yanjiu* [A Comparative Study of "Master Sun's Art of War" and "On War"], Beijing 2003, p. 209.

[12] Yi Mou, "Ba Sike yu 'sanshiliu ji' yiqi chao" ["Cisco and 'the 36 stratagems' brought together"], *QXS*, no. 2, 2004, p. 25.

[13] Deng Jianhua, *Moulüe Jingwei* [The Quintessence of Global Planning], Wuhan 1994, p. 8.

[14] Lu Yuanjun (commentary and translation), *Shuo Yuan Jin Zhu Jin Yi* [The Anecdote Park with a Modern Translation and Annotations], Taipei, 3rd ed., 1985, p. 418.

[15] This example is based on the account of the Chinese interpreter, who was present throughout the negotiations in China. Information received on March 24, 2004.

[16] Lionel Giles (translation and commentary), *Sun Tzu on the Art of War*, Shanghai/London 1910, reprinted Taipei 1964, p. 61.

[17] Zhou Lei, *Shewai Hetong Loudong, Qizha, Falü Guibi Yu Fangfan* [Loopholes, Betrayals, and Legal Evasions in Contracts with Foreign Countries, and How to Guard Against Them], Beijing 1996, p. 196.

[18] Julius H. Schoeps, "Wie viel kostet der Stephansdom?" ["How much does St. Stephen's Cathedral cost?"], in the literary supplement of *Die Zeit*, German weekly newspaper, Hamburg, October 2002; http://literaturbeilage.zeit.de, April 10, 2004.

[19] Nicolas G. Hayek, Innovation am Beispiel der schweizerischen Uhrenindustrie [Innovation Following the Example of the Swiss Watch Industry], lecture at the University of St. Gallen, Max Schmidheiny Foundation, 1993, manuscript, pp. 7–8.

[20] "Bidder's bluff," www.anecdotage.com/index.php?aid=12779, April 18, 2004.

[21] This example is based on the account of the Chinese interpreter,

who was present throughout the negotiations in China. Information received on March 24, 2004.

22 Quoted in Klaus M. Leisinger (head of the Ciba-Geigy Foundation for Cooperation with Developing Countries), "'Ruhe, man tötet': die äthiopische Hungersnot als politisches Instrument" ["'*Silence, on tue*': Famine in Ethiopia as a political tool"], *NZZ*, August 18, 1987, p. 5.

23 www.espace.ch/region/artikel/25032/artikel.html, March 31, 2004.

24 Ibid.

25 "Heidelberger Druckmaschinen," www.schoene-aktien.de/heidelberg_alte_aktien.html, March 31, 2004, p. 4.

26 Alexandra Kudelka, "Ein Leben für die Bildtechnik: Zum 100. Geburtstag von Dr.-Ing. Rudolf Hell" ["A life devoted to picture technology: The hundredth birthday of Dr. Rudolf Hell"], *PrePress*, Ratingen, no. 2, 2002, pp. 56ff.

27 www.espace.ch/region/artikel/25032/artikel.html, March 31, 2004.

28 Kudelka, "Ein Leben für die Bildtechnik," p. 56.

29 Ibid., pp. 60–1.

30 Konrad Seitz, *Die japanische Herausforderung: Deutschlands Hochtechnologie-Industrien kämpfen ums Überleben* [The Japanese Challenge: The German High-Technology Industries are Fighting for Their Lives], Stuttgart/Munich 1990, p. 329.

31 "Deutscher erfand biegsamen Stein: Auszeichnung" ["Prize-winning German invented malleable stone"], *Hamburger Abendblatt*, German daily newspaper, April 5, 2004; www.abendblatt.de/daten/2004/04/05/281142.html?prx=1, April 7, 2004.

32 "Le Grand Prix décerné à une invention allemande" ["The

Grand Prize awarded to a German invention"], *Tribune de Genève*, Swiss daily newspaper, April 5, 2004, p. 20.

[33] Lu Qiutian, *Chayi: Yi wei Zhongguo Dashi Yan Zhong De Dong-Xifang Siwei* [Differences: Eastern and Western Thought in the Eyes of a Chinese Ambassador], Shanghai 2003, p. 35.

[34] "The Homestead strike," www.pbs.org/wgbh/amex/carnegie/peopleevents/pande04.html, April 11, 2004.

[35] "Das Rockefeller-Prinzip" ["The Rockefeller principle"], www.br-online.de/jugend/quer/higru/zubehoer.html, April 2, 2004.

[36] See, in particular, Harro von Senger, *Einführung in das chinesische Recht* [Introduction to Chinese Law], Munich 1994, pp. 207ff., 245; by the same author, *Partei, Ideologie und Gesetz in der Volksrepublik China* [Party, Ideology, and Law in the People's Republic of China], Bern 1982, pp. 8ff.

[37] Gu Zengwen, "Zusammenarbeit mit den chinesischen Partnern und die interkulturelle Kommunikation im chinesischen Alltagsleben" ["Working together with Chinese partners, and intercultural communication in everyday life"], *China-Report*, Constance, no. 40, January 15, 2004, p. 7.

[38] This example is based on the account of the Chinese interpreter, who was present throughout the negotiations in China. Information received on March 24, 2004.

[39] More about this "polarity norm," typical in the People's Republic of China, in Harro von Senger, *Einführung in das chinesische Recht* [Introduction to Chinese Law], Munich 1994, pp. 297ff, and Harro von Senger, "Recent Developments in the Relations between State and Party Norms in the People's Republic of China, " *The Scope of State Power in China*, S.R. Schram (ed.), London, Hong Kong 1985, pp. 171–207.

[40] Hans Dieter Sauer, "Der lange Weg des Transrapid zum kommerziellen Start: Zögerliche Planung in Deutschland—rasche

Realisierung in Shanghai" ["The Transrapid's long journey to its commercial beginnings: Hesitant planning in Germany—rapid realization in Shanghai"], *NZZ*, July 17, 2002, p. 55.

[41] Franz Büllingen, *Die Genese der Magnetbahn Transrapid* [The Genesis of the Transrapid Magnetic Railroad], Bielefeld 1996, quoted in Sauer, "Der lange Weg des Transrapid zum kommerziellen Start," p. 55.

[42] Klaus Köncke, "Transrapid in China," *China-Report*, Constance, no. 36, January 15, 2002, p. 4.

[43] Ibid.

[44] Klaus Koch, "Auf Stelzen durch den Schlamm der Mitte: chinesische Betreiber der Magnetschwebebahn klagen über technische Probleme und fordern die rasche Weiterentwicklung" ["Walking on stilts through the middle of a swamp: The Chinese contractors on the magnetic-suspension railroad complain about technical problems and demand rapid further development"], *Süddeutsche Zeitung*, German daily newspaper, November 22/23, 2003, p. V1/1.

[45] Daniel Delheas and Frank Sieren, "Unternehmen Metrorapid: Nichts zu feiern" ["Nothing to celebrate about the Metrorapid enterprise"], *Wirtschaftswoche*, German weekly magazine, November 21, 2002, p. 70.

[46] Koch, "Auf Stelzen durch den Schlamm der Mitte," p. V1/1.

[47] Delheas and Sieren, "Unternehmen Metrorapid," p. 71.

[48] Ibid.

[49] Mao Dun, *Ziye* [Midnight], Beijing 1978, p. 50; German translation, *Schanghai im Zwielicht* [Shanghai in the Twilight], Frankfurt 1983, p. 48; English translation, *Mao Tun: Midnight*, Beijing 1979, p. 42.

ALWAYS CHANGE A WINNING TEAM

Why reinvention and change are prerequisites for business success

Peter P. Robertson

£16.99 Paperback

ISBN 981 261 800 7 (Asia & ANZ)

ISBN 0-9542829-9-X (Rest of world)

"Continuous change" is a phrase bandied about so often that it has become a cliché. Yet, if we take a look around us, we can see how difficult it is to put the idea into practice. Many companies seem to get stuck in a rut. Their rules, procedures, and power politics start to take over, and become more important in day-to-day operations than looking for new ways of serving customers or keeping costs to a minimum.

Surprisingly, it is often the most successful companies that fall into this trap. When things are going well, we relax our defenses. Is there a way out? Can a company be successful without sacrificing its adaptability?

Having spent the last two decades steeped in the issues surrounding change management and growth strategies, Peter Robertson brings extensive experience to bear in tackling these questions. He offers no quick fixes but identifies the factors that make people open to change, and shows how leaders can create the conditions to keep their organizations nimble, responsive, and effective in today's turbulent business environment.

THE RULES OF EQ

Rob Yeung

£9.99 Hardback

ISBN 981 261 812 0 (Asia & ANZ)

ISBN 1-904879-37-3 (Rest of world)

In today's demanding business world, it takes more than brains and hard work to get along. Those who succeed have another quality in common: emotional intelligence.

In this readable introduction Rob Yeung explains how to up your "EQ"—your emotional intelligence quotient—and to use it to get ahead at work. He encourages you to get to know, and control, your own emotions, to become self-directed, resilient and success-oriented. Learn how to kill those ANTs (automatic negative thoughts), and deal with setbacks as well as successes.

"Interpersonal savvy" is what you need to get on with other people, to understand what makes them tick and to get the best out of them. On a wider scale, what Yeung calls "organizational savvy" tells you how to translate this to a larger scale, to play the office politics game to your own best advantage.

The tips in this book can set you on the road to greater happiness and greater success. A higher EQ is yours for the taking.

THE RULES OF NETWORKING

Rob Yeung

£9.99 Hardback

ISBN 981 261 813 9 (Asia & ANZ)

ISBN 1-904879-38-1 (Rest of world)

Networking—an essential skill required of all bright young professionals hoping to progress in their chosen career path, yet the mere mention of the word can leave even the most confident among us tongue-tied. This book is a snappy, step-by-step alternative to traditional management tomes and is designed to steer you safely through the unpredictable battlefield of modern working life.

Rob Yeung quietens the panicky inner voice of many a reader, which cries "But I don't know anybody important," and expertly explains exactly how to network your way to the top. This easy-to-follow guide is packed with hints and tips. The relaxed and chatty tone that Yeung adopts makes this book a pleasure to read, while each step of the networking process is clearly signposted.

Would you like to get promoted? Do you want to earn more money? Did you answer yes to these questions but don't quite know how to do it? With perseverance and dedication Yeung can show you exactly how to reach your dream goals. Let's get networking!

FAQS ON MARKETING

Answered by the guru of
marketing

Philip Kotler

£9.99 Hardback

ISBN 981 261 805 8 (Asia & ANZ)

ISBN 1-904879-26-8 (Rest of world)

If you had the opportunity to ask one of the world's pre-eminent authorities on marketing one question, what would you ask? Now you don't have to decide.

FAQs on Marketing distills the essence of marketing guru Philip Kotler's wisdom and years of experience into an immensely readable question and answer format. Based on the thousands of questions Kotler has been asked over the years by clients, students, business audiences, and journalists, the book reveals the revolutionary theories of one of the profession's most revered experts, with Kotler providing insightful, thought-provoking answers to questions such as:

- What skills do marketing managers need to be successful?
- What metrics can companies use to judge marketing performance?
- What marketing strategies make sense during a recession?
- What will the marketing department of the future look like?

FAQs on Marketing is a book that you'll refer to again and again, It will forever change the way you think about marketing.